Naturally,

DELICIOUS DINNERS

Naturally,

DELICIOUS DINNERS

Danny Seo

GIBBS SMITH
TO ENRICH AND INSPIRE HUMANKIND

First Edition
25 24 23 22 21   5 4 3 2 1

PHOTO CREDITS
Photographs by Rikki Snyder pages 6, 12, 28, 30, 32, 40, 42, 45, 46, 60, 79, 80, 90, 94, 98, 101, 102, 104, 113, 120, 123, 142, 146, 157, 162, 165, 166, 171, 175, 189, 191, 192, 197, 198, 202, 204, 206, 207, 208, 210, 215.
Photographs by Jonas Jungblut front cover, pages 9, 10, 12, 38, 48, 93, 145, 172, 185, 200, 212, 216.
Photographs by Alexandra Grablewski pages 14, 16, 19, 20, 23, 24, 35, 51, 52, 55, 56, 59, 63, 64, 67, 76, 77, 85, 88, 107, 110, 114, 117, 118, 119, 136, 138, 141, 149, 150, 153, 158, 161, 168, 176, 179, 180, 182, 186, 188.
Photographs by Biz Jones pages 27, 86.
Photographs by Armando Rafael pages 34, 37, 68, 70, 72, 73, 74, 97, 124, 194.
Photographs by David Engelhardt pages 83, 108, 154, 218, 224.
Photographs by Masha Sullivan pages 127, 128, 131, 132, 135.

Published by
Gibbs Smith
P.O. Box 667
Layton, Utah 84041

1.800.835.4993 orders
www.gibbs-smith.com

Designed by Made Visible Studio
Printed and bound in China
Gibbs Smith books are printed on either recycled, 100% post-consumer waste, FSC-certified papers or on paper produced from sustainable PEFC-certified forest/controlled wood source. Learn more at www.pefc.org.

Library of Congress Cataloging-in-Publication Data

Names: Seo, Danny, author.
Title: Naturally, delicious dinners / Danny Seo.
Description: First edition. | Layton, Utah : Gibbs Smith, [2021] |
Identifiers: LCCN 2021002912 | ISBN 9781423658269 (hardcover) | ISBN 9781423658276 (epub)
Subjects: LCSH: Cooking (Natural foods)
Classification: LCC TX741 .S4655 2021 | DDC 641.3/02—dc23
LC record available at https://lccn.loc.gov/2021002912

To the Thompson Family—Dave, Karen, Kerry,

Colin, and Sydney—and the many, many, many meals

we've enjoyed together and the many more to come.

Cheers!

CONTENTS

ACKNOWLEDGMENTS

It sure takes a village to make a book, and this is no exception.

Of course, I owe a big dose of gratitude to Gibbs Smith and my editor, Michelle Branson, who had the brilliant idea to turn the "best of" recipes from the huge *Naturally, Danny Seo* archives into a beautiful series of books.

My agent I've worked with for as long as I can remember—Joy Tutela—is a fighter, opinionated, and someone I'm proud to call a fantastic friend.

The hardworking photographers who contributed to this book: Alexandra Grablewski, Rikki Snyder, David Engelhardt, Biz Jones, Armando Rafael, Jonas Jungblut, and Masha Sullivan.

HUGE BIG CHEERS to the food and prop stylists who make each image shine: Maeve Sheridan, Kristine Trevino, Nidia Cuevo, Corey Belle, Eugene Jho, and Leslie Orlandini.

A special thanks to our Culinary Director, Olivia Roszkowksi, whom I call my mad genius who can take a simple idea like "bright and happy" and churn out 100 ideas *just like that*.

Plus, everyone at the magazine who help create one issue after another (and each time better!): Sandy Soria, Alexis Cook, Mike Wilson, and all the contributing writers and everyone at RFP Corp, including my business partner in crime, Barry Rosenbloom. And to all the brand partners who have supported us from the start and continue to do so today, thank you soooo much. A big thank-you to Bob's Red Mill, Boiron, MegaFood, and Eden Foods for being with us since the first issue!

And finally, a big thank-you to all the readers. I hope these recipes bring joy to the dinner table. Live every day with beauty, truth, and goodness.

INTRODUCTION

Here's how I would like for you to use this book: if it looks good to you, make it for dinner tonight.

The definition of what's "dinner" has evolved over the past few decades. Gone is the romantic idea of sitting down at a candlelit table with others, passing around side dishes, and presenting an impressive main course that took hours to prepare. Those kinds of mealtime scenarios seem best for movies and for just a few special occasions throughout the year.

Also gone is the idea that fast food is sufficient for sustenance. Sure, throwing a frozen meal into the microwave oven is convenient, but the results are usually subpar and—in almost every case—unhealthy. Plus, takeout food is wasteful for both the wallet and the environment with all of the single-use plastic.

What's the happy middle ground? I think this book is it.

In creating my magazine *Naturally, Danny Seo* I worked with our culinary team to come up with recipe ideas that worked with my cooking ethos. First, everything has to be wholesome, healthy, and vegetarian. Second, the number of ingredients had to be kept to a minimum, but not so stripped down that the ideas felt silly or basic. And lastly, they couldn't take a long time to *physically* prepare. Leaving a one-pot dish in the oven to bake for an hour? Sure, that's fine, because I can walk away and entertain myself with a game of Scrabble on my phone. Hand spiralizing vegetables for forty-five minutes straight? No, we need to find an easier way.

After six years, and over 1,000 recipes, we have found a happy place where the cooking is easy, healthy, delicious, and foolproof. I promise you, these recipes have been perfected and tested within an inch of their casserole-baked life! And, with *Naturally, Delicious Dinners*, I pored through the pages and picked my all-star favorites from the magazine's archives. The winners are delicious, and some are quite unusual. And many can be doubled or tripled to feed a crowd. A few use ingredients you may have never tried, such as nutritional yeast, which you'll use to make our carrot risotto (page 182). A few use something common—like coffee—as a star ingredient in dishes to make something new, such as the Coffee-Rubbed Portobello Fajitas (page 66). And, yes, there are lots of options for vegans, those avoiding gluten, and a few for those dedicated to a keto-friendly lifestyle.

Even warm twisted breadsticks can be a fabulous dinner. Just add a simple seasonal salad with a homemade dressing and you've got a better version of the unlimited breadsticks and salad you'll find at that restaurant chain. But instead of all-you-*can*-eat, these will be more all-you-*want*-to-eat.

Cheers and enjoy!

—Danny Seo

BREAD &
MORE BREAD

If you can master one or two of these "scratch" bread recipes, your friends and family are going to think you're a master chef. For a lot of people, the thought of turning something doughy into crispy, flaky, piping-hot bread seems like an impossible task. But it's not: all you have to do is combine some wet ingredients and dry ingredients together and slather on some tasty ingredients to make anything from biscuits to rolls to cheese straws to pizza.

I love bready main dishes for dinner. Warm bread is incredibly satiating, and it's a crowd-pleaser. For too long, we've made anything "bread" demonic when it comes to healthy eating. Sure, a loaf of white bread from the supermarket is devoid of nutrition and can be an easy path toward getting a belly. But breads using alternative flours, real wholesome ingredients, and a few hacks from our *Naturally* culinary team can be really good for you and really delicious, too!

Nearly every recipe in this section makes the bread course the star of the dish. Add some cooked hearty veggies, a salad, or the protein of your choice to round out the meal.

Pumpkin Rosemary Biscuits

MAKES 16 BISCUITS

These biscuits call for an unusual ingredient: sprouted wheat flour. This product is made from wheat kernels that are soaked and left to germinate to turn into a plant. After sprouting, they are dried and then ground into traditional flour. The reason sprouted wheat flour is healthier than conventional is that it not only contains less starch (so it's easier to digest) but it's also loaded with vitamins such as iron, zinc, and magnesium. If you can't find sprouted flour, just use organic whole-grain flour.

GATHER

BISCUITS

½	cup (1 stick) salted grass-fed butter
4	sprigs rosemary
2 ½	cups sprouted wheat flour, more for dusting surface
1	tablespoon baking powder
¾	cup pumpkin purée
¾	cup Greek yogurt

ROSEMARY BUTTER

½	cup (1 stick) salted grass-fed butter
2	sprigs rosemary, stemmed

MAKE IT

FOR THE BISCUITS

Preheat oven to 375°F. Line a baking tray with parchment paper.

Melt butter in a small pan over medium heat and cook for 2–3 minutes, or until brown butter forms. Chill in freezer, reserving 2 tablespoons to brush biscuit tops.

Stem rosemary and set aside half for garnish. Mince remaining rosemary (1 tablespoon).

In a medium bowl, combine minced rosemary, flour, and baking powder. Cut chilled brown butter into flour mixture using a fork until flour is crumbly.

In a separate bowl, mix together pumpkin and yogurt. Gently fold in the pumpkin-yogurt mixture into the flour mixture, taking care not to overmix.

Dust a clean work surface and rolling pin with flour and roll dough into a 1-inch-thick rectangle. Fold dough in half and roll again, repeating process 4 times.

Cut dough into 3-inch squares. Transfer to prepared baking tray. Press reserved rosemary onto biscuit tops and brush with reserved butter.

Bake for 20–25 minutes, or until golden and firm to the touch. Serve with rosemary butter.

FOR THE BUTTER

Cut butter into small pieces and place in a small bowl to soften.

Mince rosemary (1 tablespoon) and fold into butter mixture.

Place softened rosemary butter mixture onto the center of a sheet of parchment paper and roll to form a log. Chill and cut into rounds.

Cauliflower Pizza Crust with Carrot-Top Pesto and Rainbow Carrots

MAKES 1 MEDIUM PIZZA

Okay, this is not traditional pizza dough in any sense: It's a cauliflower crust pizza that's free of any gluten. But if you've ever made a cauliflower crust pizza recipe at home and were disappointed with how soggy or flimsy the crust turned out, please give this one a try. We worked hard to perfect the cauliflower crust "dough" into one that binds well, has a crunch, and can hold up to whatever toppings you slather on top.

GATHER

HONEY-FENNEL ROASTED CARROTS

- 1 bunch rainbow carrots, greens reserved
- 1 teaspoon fennel seeds
- 1 tablespoon raw honey
- 2 tablespoons olive oil
- ½ teaspoon sea salt

CARROT-TOP PESTO

- Reserved carrot tops, rinsed
- 1 cup Greek yogurt
- 2 tablespoons miso
- 2 cloves garlic
- ¼ teaspoon sea salt
- 2 tablespoons olive oil

CAULIFLOWER PIZZA CRUST

- 3 tablespoons olive oil, more to grease baking tray
- 1 large yellow onion, diced (about 3 cups)
- 1½ teaspoons sea salt
- 1 head cauliflower, "riced" in a food processor or using the large side of a box grater (or 4 cups fresh/frozen cauliflower "rice")
- 2 sprigs oregano
- ¼ teaspoon red chili flakes
- 1 organic egg

MAKE IT

FOR THE CARROTS

Preheat oven to 400°F.

Cut carrots in half lengthwise.

Slightly chop fennel seeds with sharp knife.

Toss carrots with fennel, honey, oil, and salt and spread onto baking tray. Roast for 20–25 minutes, or until carrots are golden and softened.

FOR THE PESTO

Bring a small pot of water to a boil.

Add carrot tops to boiling water for 10 seconds or until wilted. Drain and cool under cold running water. Squeeze out liquid well and finely chop (approximately 1 cup).

Add greens, yogurt, miso, garlic, and salt to a blender and purée until smooth. Transfer to bowl and stir in olive oil.

FOR THE CRUST

Preheat oven to 400°F. Warm olive oil in a large pan.

Warm olive oil in a large pan over medium heat. Add onion to the pan, along with the salt. Cook for 5–7 minutes or until softened. Add cauliflower and cook for 10 minutes, stirring frequently, or until moisture evaporates.

Remove stems and chop oregano (2 teaspoons). Add to cauliflower mixture along with chili flakes. Transfer mixture into shallow pan and cool for 15 minutes.

While the mixture cools, line a baking tray with parchment paper and grease with olive oil.

Beat egg and fold into cauliflower mixture to form dough (about 2½ cups).

Spread dough into a thin 12-inch circle. Transfer to prepared baking tray.

Bake crust for 30–40 minutes until firm and golden. (Note: if crust is not firm enough to handle, reduce heat to 275°F. Bake for another 15 minutes.)

Top cauliflower crust with pesto and honey-fennel roasted carrots, cut into slices, and serve warm.

Paleo Pizza Biscuits

MAKES 12 BISCUITS

Because it's high-fat, high-protein, and gluten-free, almond flour is a great grain-free alternative flour to use for baking. And while these are Paleo-friendly biscuits, they are also just darn good ones, too. By the way, you can also make your own almond flour at home: just use blanched almonds and toss them into a blender or food processor until it's a powdery flour consistency. Yes, it really is that easy.

GATHER

- 3 cups almond flour
- ½ cup ground flaxseed
- ¼ cup nutritional yeast
- 2 teaspoons sea salt
- ½ teaspoon red chili flakes
- 1 tablespoon garlic powder
- 5 sprigs oregano, stemmed and leaves roughly chopped
- ¼ cup sun-dried tomatoes, chopped
- ¾ cup refined coconut oil
- ¼ cup filtered water

MAKE IT

Preheat oven to 350°F.

Stir together almond flour, ground flaxseed, nutritional yeast, salt, red chili flakes, and garlic powder in a medium bowl.

Stir oregano (approximately 2 tablespoons) into almond flour mixture. Stir in sun-dried tomatoes.

Add coconut oil and water to mixture and use hands to evenly distribute until dough forms. Set aside and allow dough to rest for 10 minutes.

Line a baking tray with parchment paper. Use a ¼-cup measure to mold batter into a biscuit shape. Place onto baking tray and repeat with remaining batter.

Bake for 15 minutes, or until biscuits are cooked through and golden. Allow to cool for 10 minutes before serving.

Vegan "Cheese" Straws with Garlic "Caesar" Dip

MAKES 12 STRAWS AND ⅔ CUP DRESSING

This plant-based recipe makes two different types of dairy-free cheese profiles. Nutritional yeast, which is rich in B vitamins, gives the straws a natural cheesy note, and the cashews help bring out the familiar Caesar dressing flavor in the dip. If you want the sticks to be more crispy than doughy, just roll out the dough thinner before baking.

GATHER

"CHEESE" STRAWS

1	cup sprouted wheat flour
⅓	cup nutritional yeast
1	teaspoon ground black pepper, more for garnish
1	teaspoon sea salt
¼	cup olive oil, more to brush
⅓	cup filtered water

GARLIC "CAESAR" DIP

½	cup cashews
1	tablespoon nutritional yeast
½	teaspoon sea salt
2	tablespoons lemon juice
2	cloves garlic
⅓	cup filtered water

MAKE IT

FOR THE "CHEESE" STRAWS

Preheat oven to 350°F. Line a baking tray with parchment paper.

Add flour, nutritional yeast, pepper, and salt to a bowl and stir to combine. Stream olive oil into flour mixture and use hands to evenly distribute. Repeat process with water and knead with hands until dough forms.

Divide mixture into 12 pieces and cover to prevent dough from drying out.

Roll out each piece into a long strip, approximately 12 inches long. Fold each strip in half and twist together into a spiral by gently pinching the end where the two pieces meet and braiding it in one direction. Roll gently to seal the two strands together.

Place spirals onto prepared baking tray, and brush with olive oil. Bake for 15 minutes, or until golden and crunchy and serve with Garlic "Caesar" Dip. Garnish with ground black pepper.

FOR THE DIP

While the "cheese" straws bake, cover cashews with hot water for 10 minutes to soften.

Drain and rinse soaked cashews and place in blender with nutritional yeast, salt, lemon juice, garlic, and water.

Process until smooth, and refrigerate until ready to serve.

Seeded Protein Pull-Apart Dinner Rolls

MAKES 12 MEDIUM-SIZE ROLLS

These rolls are loaded with seeds, and that's a good thing. Seeds are high in fiber, vitamin E, minerals, and healthy monounsaturated fats, and they also add a nice crunch to these soft, pillowy rolls. When baking these, make sure your rolls are not overcrowded in your baking pan, as they can merge and form one giant bread-like structure.

GATHER

ROLLS
- 1¼ cups warm filtered water, divided
- 1 tablespoon dry active yeast
- 1 tablespoon raw honey
- 3 cups whole-wheat flour
- 1 teaspoon sea salt
- ⅓ cup pea protein powder
- ¼ cup olive oil, more to grease baking dish

SEEDED COATING
- 1 tablespoon sesame seeds
- 1 tablespoon poppy seeds
- 2 tablespoons pumpkin seeds

MAKE IT

Preheat oven to 350°F.

Form a sponge by adding ½ cup warm water, dry active yeast, honey, and ¼ cup whole-wheat flour to a large mixing bowl. Cover bowl and allow mixture to sit in a warm location for 15 minutes, or until foamy.

In a separate bowl, stir together the remaining flour, salt, and protein powder. Add remaining water and olive oil.

If using a stand mixer with a dough hook attachment, combine the yeast and flour mixture. Knead the dough on medium speed for 2–3 minutes, or until it starts pulling from the edges of the bowl. If mixing dough manually, add flour mixture to the yeast mixture in a bowl and mix with a spatula. Transfer mixture to a floured surface and knead for 8–10 minutes, or until a firm and smooth dough forms.

Place dough back into bowl, cover, and allow to rise for 30 minutes in a warm location. Grease a 10-inch pan or similarly sized baking dish.

Lay dough out onto a cutting board, and, using a knife, cut dough into quarters. Cut each quarter piece of dough into thirds, and roll each into a log. Roll the log into itself to form a circular roll.

Place each type of seed in a small dish. Dip the top of each roll in either sesame, poppy, or pumpkin seeds and place each roll next to each other in the baking dish. The rolls should be touching, but not overcrowded.

Cover dish and allow rolls to rise for 15–30 minutes. Transfer to oven and bake for 25–30 minutes, or until a toothpick comes out clean.

Savory Feta and Black Olive Scones

MAKES 18 SCONES

These savory scones are not only plant-based, but they also use just six ingredients! This recipe uses spelt flour, which is considered an "ancient grain" due to the fact its DNA hasn't changed much in comparison to today's modern-day wheat. And while it has gluten, many find spelt to be a much more easily digestible grain.

GATHER

- 2 cups spelt flour, more to dust cutting board
- 2 teaspoons baking powder
- 4 tablespoons refined coconut oil, chilled
- ⅔ cup unsweetened almond milk, more to brush
- 4 ounces feta (¾ cup), crumbled
- ¼ cup pitted black olives, chopped

MAKE IT

Preheat oven to 350°F. Line a baking tray with parchment paper.

Stir together flour and baking powder in a medium bowl.

Add chilled coconut oil to the flour mixture, and use a fork to incorporate the oil for 1 minute. The flour should take on a crumbly texture.

In a separate bowl, gently fold together the milk, feta, and olives.

Pour the milk mixture into the flour mixture, and stir gently for 10–20 seconds, or just until combined and a dough forms. Take care not to overmix.

Dust a flat, clean surface with flour and place dough onto surface.

Using a rolling pin, roll mixture into a 1-inch-thick rectangle, and use a sharp knife or pastry cutter to cut dough into triangles or squares. Brush tops of the scones with almond milk.

Place scones in a single layer on the prepared baking tray. Bake for 15–18 minutes, or until lightly golden and firm to the touch.

Zucchini-and-Walnut Spelt Bread

MAKES ABOUT 10 TO 12 GENEROUS SLICES

My good friend Melanie Hansche has worked at some of the best culinary publications around, including *Donna Hay* and *Food & Wine*. She and her husband opened an Australian-inspired café in rural Pennsylvania called Tucker that's become a go-to destination for East Coast foodies. This recipe for their zucchini-and-walnut spelt bread is a winner and the right balance of something sweet but not dessert-like. If you pair this with a crunchy salad, you've got a perfect, fresh, and light dinner.

GATHER

3 organic eggs
1½ cups coconut sugar
1 cup olive oil, more for greasing the pan
2 cups spelt flour, more for flouring the pan
½ teaspoon baking powder
2 teaspoons baking soda
2 teaspoons ground cinnamon
1 teaspoon table salt
2 cups grated zucchini (2 medium zucchini)
1 cup coarsely chopped walnuts
2 teaspoons vanilla extract

MAKE IT

Preheat oven to 350°F. Grease and flour 1 large (10½ x 4½-inch) or 2 small (5½ x 3-inch) loaf pans.

In a bowl, beat the eggs, sugar, and olive oil with an electric mixer until light and smooth, about 5 minutes.

Stir in the flour, baking powder, baking soda, cinnamon, and salt until combined. Add the zucchini, walnuts, and vanilla; mix well to combine.

Pour the batter into the prepared pans. Bake for 50–60 minutes or until a skewer inserted into the center comes out clean. Cool on a wire rack.

Moroccan-Spiced Chickpea Skillet Bread

MAKES 8 SLICES

What could be easier? Toss the ingredients into a blender and bake in a sizzling-hot cast iron skillet. Not only is this gluten-free skillet bread delicious, it's impressive when sliced hot at the table, too. If you don't have harissa, switch to one teaspoon each of sage, garlic, and nutritional yeast, and it'll give you a fun play on traditional garlic bread.

GATHER

FOR THE BREAD
1½	cups chickpea flour
1½	cups filtered water
1¾	teaspoons sea salt, divided
6	tablespoons olive oil, divided
¼	cup za'atar
1	cup chickpeas
1	teaspoon harissa

FOR THE TOPPINGS
½	cup plain yogurt of choice
½	cup mint leaves
1	seeded pomegranate

MAKE IT

Preheat oven to 450°F.

In a blender, process flour, filtered water, 1 ½ teaspoons sea salt, and 4 tablespoons of olive oil, until smooth. Stir in za'atar. Allow batter to rest for 5 minutes.

Drain chickpeas and gently pat dry. Heat up 12–15-inch cast iron skillet over medium heat. Add remaining oil and chickpeas and crisp for 5 minutes on high heat, stirring occasionally. Transfer to bowl and season with harissa and remaining salt.

Pour batter into same hot cast iron pan and transfer to oven for 15 minutes or until golden and the center is cooked through.

Top with crisped chickpeas, yogurt, mint leaves, and pomegranate seeds, to taste.

Purple Cauliflower Toast With White Bean Spread and Caper-Raisin Relish

MAKES ABOUT
10 OPEN-FACED
SANDWICHES

The purple cauliflower here is really just for a wow factor. If you can't find purple, any color will do just fine. You can also dissect this recipe to make new sides and sauces. The white bean spread is a great dip and spread to keep on hand in the fridge. Or the relish can top veggies or protein to give it a little extra zing.

GATHER

ROASTED CAULIFLOWER

1 small purple cauliflower
2 tablespoons olive oil
¼ teaspoon sea salt

WHITE BEAN SPREAD

3 tablespoons olive oil
4 cloves garlic, sliced
   Pinch of red chili flakes
¾ teaspoon sea salt
1 sprig rosemary leaves, minced (1 teaspoon)
1 (15.5-ounce) can white beans, drained and rinsed
3 tablespoons lemon juice

CAPER-RAISIN RELISH

¼ cup capers
½ cup golden raisins
2 teaspoons lemon zest
1 tablespoon olive oil
1 scallion, sliced (approximately ¼ cup)

TO SERVE

1 loaf sourdough, cut into ¼-inch slices and charred lightly on stovetop, or toasted
½ teaspoon freshly ground black pepper

MAKE IT

FOR THE CAULIFLOWER

Preheat oven to 325 °F. Line a baking tray with parchment paper.

Cut cauliflower into large florets, and cut florets into slices to showcase cauliflower cross-sections. Reserve leftovers pieces for future uses, such as soups or stir-fries.

Brush cauliflower pieces with olive oil, season with salt, and roast for 15 minutes.

FOR THE SPREAD

While the cauliflower roasts, make the spread and relish. Add olive oil to a medium sauté pan and heat over medium heat. Add garlic and allow to cook for 30 seconds, taking care not to brown.

Stir in the chili flakes, salt, and minced rosemary and cook for additional 10 seconds. Fold in white beans, and turn off heat.

Add bean mixture along with lemon juice to food processor and process until smooth.

FOR THE RELISH

Add capers, raisins, lemon zest, oil, and sliced scallion to a small bowl and stir to combine. Allow to sit for 5 minutes to marinate before serving.

TO SERVE

Spread some puréed bean mixture onto each piece of toast.

Scatter caper-raisin relish on top of bean mixture, followed by roasted cauliflower pieces, and freshly ground black pepper.

Grilled Chickpea Flatbread with Cashew "Ricotta," Grilled Zucchini, and Mint

SERVES 4

A chickpea can do a lot more than top salads or be made into hummus. The low-calorie legume is incredibly versatile, and this recipe really shows the possibilities. Try the flatbread recipe on its own and add whatever toppings you want if you want to speed up this recipe start-to-finish. Or, double the ricotta so you can use half for the flatbread and the rest for a sandwich spread tomorrow.

GATHER

CHICKPEA FLATBREAD

2	tablespoons olive oil, more for brushing
2	cups chickpea flour
3	cups filtered water
1	teaspoon sea salt
3	sprigs oregano leaves, chopped
½	teaspoon freshly ground black pepper

CASHEW "RICOTTA"

2	cups cashews, soaked
1	lemon, zested and juiced
1	clove garlic
3	tablespoons miso
½	teaspoon sea salt
3	tablespoons refined coconut oil, melted

TOPPINGS

2	zucchini, cut into small wedges
2	tablespoons olive oil
1	teaspoon freshly cracked black pepper
½	teaspoon sea salt
¼	cup pitted black olives, cut in half lengthwise
3	sprigs mint, for garnish

MAKE IT

FOR THE FLATBREAD

Line a 12-inch baking tray with parchment paper and brush with olive oil.

To a medium pot, add the chickpea flour and whisk in the water, oil, and salt until smooth. Cook over medium heat, stirring constantly for 10 minutes or until thick paste forms and mixture pulls slightly from the side of the pot. Add the oregano and pepper.

Working quickly, pour the batter onto the prepared tray and spread to an approximately ⅛-inch thickness.

Cool mixture in refrigerator for 15–20 minutes.

Cut the chickpea "flatbread" into crostini-like pieces and brush with olive oil.

Preheat grill pan over medium-high heat and grill flatbread for 2 minutes per side, or until grill marks appear.

FOR THE "RICOTTA"

Drain and rinse soaked cashews and add to food processor with lemon zest, lemon juice, garlic, miso, salt, and melted coconut oil.

Process until smooth, adding a few tablespoons of water, if necessary, to thin mixture.

FOR THE TOPPINGS

Toss the cut zucchini with oil, pepper, and salt.

Preheat grill pan over medium heat and cook the zucchini for 2 minutes per side, or until grill marks appear.

Add a dollop of cashew "ricotta" onto each flatbread and top with grilled zucchini, black olives, and mint.

Millet Skillet Cornbread

MAKES 12 SLICES

Millet is an ancient grain and has been around for more than 7,000 years. Yes, you've seen it in birdseed mixes, but it's worth picking up a bag at the supermarket to add into your diet, too. The naturally gluten-free grain is high in protein, fiber, B vitamins, and magnesium and has a mildly sweet and nutty flavor profile that makes it perfect for this cornbread.

GATHER

- 2 tablespoons canola oil
- ½ cup millet
- 1½ cups filtered water
- 1¼ teaspoons salt, divided
- ½ cup (1 stick) grass-fed butter, melted
- 2 cups buttermilk
- ¼ cup maple syrup
- 2 cups cornmeal
- ½ teaspoon baking soda

MAKE IT

Preheat oven to 350°F. Grease a 10-inch cast iron skillet with canola oil. Set aside.

In a 2-quart pot, combine millet, water, and ¼ teaspoon salt. Bring millet to simmer, lower heat to lowest setting, and cook until all water is absorbed, approximately 20 minutes.

In a bowl, whisk together melted butter, buttermilk, and syrup. Stir in cooked millet. Set aside.

In separate bowl, whisk together cornmeal, baking soda, and remaining salt. Mix wet ingredients into dry until just combined.

Over medium heat, heat the skillet. Pour batter into pan and transfer to oven. Bake until lightly golden and a toothpick inserted in the center comes out clean.

Coconut-Flour Flatbread with Summer-Herb Chutney

MAKES 4 FLATBREADS

You might have a hard time finding psyllium husks at the grocery store, so follow my advice—go to the drugstore. It's an all-natural dietary supplement, but it's also a great ingredient to use for thickening, or as an egg replacer. Have fun with the chutney—if you have an abundance of mint or parsley in the garden, throw it in!

GATHER

- ½ cup coconut flour
- ¼ cup ground psyllium husks
- 1 teaspoon sea salt, divided
- 1 small bunch cilantro, stemmed and leaves chopped (approximately 2 cups), divided
- 1 (13.5-ounce) can coconut cream, divided
- ½ cup filtered water
- 2 tablespoons peeled and minced ginger
- 1 jalapeño, minced

MAKE IT

Add flour, psyllium husks, and ½ teaspoon sea salt to a medium bowl.

Add ¼ cup cilantro leaves to flour mixture, along with ¼ cup coconut cream and ½ cup filtered water. Stir to form dough and allow to rest, covered, for 5 minutes.

Meanwhile, make the chutney: Add remaining sea salt, cilantro, and coconut cream with ginger and jalapeño to a separate bowl. Stir to combine.

Divide dough into 4 equal sections and use rolling pin or hands to press into ¼-inch-thick circles.

Warm a nonstick pan over medium heat. Cook each flatbread for 2 minutes per side, or until slightly charred and cooked through.

Serve with the herb chutney.

Savory Goat Cheese Crostata

SERVES 4

I adore the rustic feel of a crostata. The dough is quite forgiving. Just be sure you use parchment paper when you roll it to prevent sticking. The addition of quinoa flour here adds a nutty, coarse texture to the crust. This is protein-rich, too, with seventeen grams of protein per serving.

GATHER

THE CRUST

- ¾ cup white whole-wheat flour, more for dusting
- ½ cup quinoa flour
- ¼ cup finely grated Parmesan cheese
- 1 teaspoon kosher salt
- ½ cup (1 stick) unsalted grass-fed butter, chilled, cut into 1-inch pieces
- 1 large organic egg, lightly whisked

THE FILLING

- 4 ounces goat cheese, softened
- 1 teaspoon lemon zest
- 1 teaspoon lemon juice
- ¼ cup chopped fresh chives
- 2 teaspoons chopped fresh mint
- ½ teaspoon fresh thyme leaves
- ¼ teaspoon kosher salt, more for seasoning asparagus
- ⅛ teaspoon freshly ground black pepper
- ½ cup shelled fresh peas
- ½ bunch asparagus (about ½ pound), trimmed
- 1 teaspoon extra virgin olive oil

MAKE IT

In the bowl of a food processor, pulse the flours, Parmesan, and salt. Add butter and pulse again several times until coarse crumbs develop. Then add the egg and run for 15–20 seconds, or until a ball of dough forms. Pat the dough into a 5-inch disk and cover with plastic wrap. Put the dough in the freezer for 10 minutes.

Meanwhile, make the filling: Preheat the oven to 400°F. In a bowl, mix the goat cheese with the lemon zest and juice, chives, mint, thyme, salt, and pepper. Set aside.

Bring a small saucepan of water to a boil and add the peas. Cook for 2–3 minutes, or until just tender. Drain, coarsely mash, and set aside. In another bowl, toss the asparagus with the olive oil and a good sprinkling of kosher salt.

Place the chilled dough on a piece of parchment paper, and, using a rolling pin, roll out the dough into a 12-inch round, dusting with wheat flour as needed to prevent sticking. Transfer the dough round, with its parchment paper, to a baking tray.

Spread the goat cheese mixture carefully on the dough round. Gently mash the peas into the goat cheese and top with the asparagus. Fold the edges of the dough up around the asparagus, creating a 1-inch border. Brush edges of the crostata with olive oil, and bake for 35–40 minutes, or until the crust is golden and crispy.

ALL-STAR VEGGIES

While the idea of cooking vegetables to be the main star of the dinner table isn't new at all to vegetarians, it is a trend that's growing in restaurants and even with meat eaters, too.

In the Spring 2020 issue of *Naturally, Danny Seo* we visited the rising-star chef Garrett Benedict, who opened a wildly popular restaurant called G-Love in Portland, Oregon. As a magazine editor, I know that many food trends start in Portland, and I wanted to be one of the first publications to bring Garrett into the limelight. At G-Love, he created a "reverse steakhouse," which means produce shines in vegetable-driven entrées, and a small selection of proteins play supporting roles as side dishes. Benedict's goal is to create something with a smaller carbon footprint that's better for the planet, better for people's health, and something that adheres to the credence that every little thing you can do to combat global warming counts. Besides, he adds, "There's a lot more room for creativity when working with vegetables. It's simple to make a cut of steak taste delicious, but it's more difficult when you're working with broccoli, cabbage, or cauliflower. And for me, when it's more challenging, it's more rewarding."

And it's Garrett's obsession with veggies that has us thinking we can do the same here. We're not talking big salads or baked potatoes in this chapter. We're thinking much bigger.

Winter Root Vegetables with Date Couscous

SERVES 4

This dish really is perfect for the winter season when an abundance of fresh vegetables at the farmer's market is at a minimum. When making the couscous, be creative: add dried fruit for an extra dose of sweetness. And try mixing warm and spicy seasonings together such as black pepper and cinnamon for more warmth and a deeper flavor that's perfect on a cold winter day.

GATHER

ROOT VEGETABLES

1 bunch rainbow carrots (with carrot tops, if available)

1 acorn squash

1 tablespoon ground cumin

1 tablespoon ground cinnamon

½ teaspoon freshly ground black pepper

3 tablespoons olive oil

1 teaspoon sea salt

1 lemon

¾ cup pitted green olives

DATE COUSCOUS

2 cups couscous

½ cup pitted dates, chopped

2 ¼ cups filtered water

1 teaspoon sea salt
Reserved carrot tops, chopped (about ¼ cup) (optional), for garnish

MAKE IT

FOR THE ROOT VEGETABLES

Preheat oven to 350°F. Place baking tray in oven while preheating the oven.

Peel and cut carrots into quarters, leaving a bit of the green attached. Save some carrot tops for garnish, if available.

Cut squash into 1-inch rings, discarding seeds.

Toss vegetables in cumin, cinnamon, pepper, olive oil, and sea salt.

Line heated baking tray with parchment paper, and spread vegetables into a single layer. Bake for 20 minutes.

Thinly slice the lemon, discarding any seeds, and stir into vegetables along with olives, and roast for additional 10 minutes.

FOR THE COUSCOUS

Meanwhile, make the couscous: Add couscous to a bowl. Add dates to couscous.

Boil filtered water and then pour over couscous mixture. Add salt. Cover and allow to rehydrate for 10 minutes. Fluff with a fork.

Serve vegetables warm on top of couscous, and garnish with chopped carrot tops, if using.

Chipotle BBQ Pulled Carrot Sloppy Joe Sliders

MAKES 16 SLIDERS

When you make your own BBQ sauce—which is much easier than you might think—you can control the spice and sweetness level. Any leftover sauce can be stored in an airtight jar in the refrigerator to be used later. Also, sweet potatoes and squash are great alternatives to carrots.

GATHER

3	large carrots, peeled and spiralized or shredded (approximately 4 cups)
1	yellow onion, thinly sliced
1	small purple cabbage, shredded (approximately 2 cups)
1½	teaspoons sea salt
¼	cup olive oil
¼	cup tomato paste
¼	cup maple syrup
1	teaspoon chipotle powder
2	teaspoons garlic powder
1	tablespoon apple cider vinegar
½	teaspoon sea salt
½	cup filtered water
16	slider brioche buns, or buns of choice

MAKE IT

Preheat oven to 450°F. Line a baking tray with parchment paper.

Toss and massage each vegetable separately with salt and olive oil. Spread each vegetable onto prepared tray, keeping them separate, and roast for 15 minutes. Toss each section and cook for additional 10 minutes.

For sauce, in a small pan, combine the tomato paste, syrup, chipotle powder, garlic powder, vinegar, sea salt, and filtered water. Bring to a simmer and allow to gently bubble for 10 minutes or until thickened.

Split slider buns, and toast in oven for 3–5 minutes.

Place roasted cabbage in a bowl. Pour sauce over carrots and onions and toss until combined. Place ¼ cup carrot mixture on each bun and top with ¼ cup roasted red cabbage. Serve warm.

Roasted Spaghetti Squash Winter Primavera

SERVES 2 TO 4

Spaghetti squash is a low-carb alternative to pasta, and it's a great dish to roast if you're trying to lose a few pounds. It's high in fiber and low in calories, too, so it'll also help with your digestive health and calorie intake.

GATHER

- ¾ cup cashews
- 8 shallots
- 1 spaghetti squash, cut in half lengthwise
- 1 bunch fresh sage, leaves only
- 3 tablespoons olive oil, more for garnish
- 1½ teaspoons sea salt, divided
- ¼ cup hazelnuts
- ½ cup filtered water
- ½ teaspoon freshly ground black pepper, more for garnish

MAKE IT

Soak cashews in cold water and set aside.

Preheat oven to 350°F, and line a baking tray with parchment paper.

With root still attached, cut shallots in half lengthwise and peel.

Coat the squash, sage leaves, and shallots with olive oil and sprinkle with 1 teaspoon of the salt. Place the squash halves, cut side up, on the lined tray and add the sage and shallots to the tray around the squash. Make sure sage leaves are laid flat in single layer. Bake for 10 minutes.

Remove sage leaves from oven and set aside. Remove shallots after an additional 10 minutes and set aside. Continue to cook squash for another 15–20 minutes, or until tender. Add hazelnuts to tray for last 5 minutes of roasting.

Drain cashews and place in blender along with filtered water. Trim half of the shallots and place in blender, along with remaining ½ teaspoon sea salt, and pepper. Blend until smooth.

Remove skins of hazelnuts by rubbing on a strainer. Use whole, halved, or chopped.

Use a fork to scrape the squash interior, but leave in squash shell.

Plate squash halves, and top with roasted shallot-cashew cream, hazelnuts, and crisped sage leaves. Garnish with freshly ground black pepper and olive oil.

Winter Vegetable Fajitas with Roasted Carrot "Queso"

MAKES 8 FAJITAS

The carrot "queso" is a nice hummus-like addition to give these fajitas a burst of flavor and some "meat" to the dish. The queso can be made by itself for a dip, too, and is excellent all on its own with some sautéed veggies with tofu as a main meal.

GATHER
- 3 medium carrots, peeled
- 2 sweet potatoes, peeled
- 1 bunch Lacinato kale
- 2 tablespoons fajita seasoning
- 3 tablespoons olive oil
- 3 teaspoons sea salt, divided
- 8 medium flour tortillas
- 1 cup filtered water
- 3 tablespoons nutritional yeast
- 4 cloves garlic
- 2 limes

MAKE IT
Preheat oven to 375°F and line a baking tray with parchment paper.

Slice the carrots (approximately 3 cups). Dice the sweet potatoes (approximately 4 cups). Remove stems and chop kale (approximately 4 cups). Massage kale for 1 minute.

Toss vegetables separately using fajita seasoning, olive oil, and 1 teaspoon salt, and place them in their own sections on baking tray.

Bake for 15 minutes, toss, and cook for additional 5 minutes or until vegetables are cooked through. Place tortillas in warm oven to heat.

Meanwhile, make the "queso": Blend the carrots with water, remaining 2 teaspoons salt, nutritional yeast, garlic cloves, and zest and juice of 1 lime.

Cut remaining lime into wedges.

Spread carrot "queso" onto each tortilla. Top with sweet potatoes and kale, and serve with a lime wedge.

Sweet Potato and Garlicky Kale Tacos with Chipotle Crema

MAKES 8 TO 10 TACOS

These tacos aren't spicy, but they're full of cumin and garlic goodness. The dairy-free chipotle crema adds a little heat but also some citrus zing from the lime and lime zest. I like to top these tacos with sliced avocados, pickled red onions, and freshly chopped cilantro.

GATHER

CHIPOTLE CREMA

- ½ cup Vegenaise or other plant-based mayonnaise
- ½ cup plain almond yogurt
- 1 lime, juiced
- 2 teaspoons lime zest
- ½ teaspoon chipotle powder
- ¼ teaspoon ground cumin
  Salt to taste

SWEET POTATOES

- 3 medium sweet potatoes, peeled and cut into ¼-inch cubes
- 2 teaspoons ground cumin
- ½ teaspoon ground cinnamon
- ½ teaspoon ground paprika
- 1 teaspoon granulated garlic
- 1 teaspoon salt
  Freshly ground black pepper to taste
- 5 tablespoons avocado oil

GARLICKY KALE

- 2 tablespoons avocado oil
- 5 to 6 large Lacinato kale leaves, stemmed and finely chopped
  Salt to taste
- 2 cloves garlic, minced
- ½ lime
- 4 tablespoons roughly chopped cilantro
- 8 to 10 tortillas of choice

MAKE IT

FOR THE CREMA

Mix all the ingredients together in a small bowl and chill in the fridge until ready to serve.

FOR THE SWEET POTATOES

Preheat the oven to 400°F.

In a large mixing bowl toss the sweet potatoes with the cumin, cinnamon, paprika, garlic, salt, pepper, and oil. Mix well. Transfer to a large baking tray.

Bake on the middle rack for 35–40 minutes, stirring occasionally, until the potatoes are brown and fork tender. While the sweet potatoes are in the oven, cook the kale.

FOR THE KALE

In a medium pan over medium heat, add the oil and then the kale and salt and cook for 7–9 minutes until wilted, stirring frequently. Stir in the garlic and cook for another 2 minutes. Remove from heat. Squeeze the lime over the kale and stir.

When the potatoes are done, place the baking tray over a burner on your cook top on low heat. Add the kale to the sweet potatoes and stir until everything is well combined. Stir in the cilantro and turn off the heat.

Assemble the tacos and place a dollop of chipotle crema on top of each.

Poached Eggs on Black Rice with Spicy Broccoli and Kimchi

SERVES 4

Did you know eggs give a serotonin boost while kimchi, a fermented food, is chock-full of probiotics, which have been linked to reducing social anxiety? Brain-healthy broccoli helps to slow cognitive decline. A little drizzle of CBD oil over the eggs right before serving also works well here. How calm.

GATHER

- 1 cup dried black rice
- 2 cups filtered water
- 1 teaspoon kosher salt, more for seasoning
- 3 tablespoons apple cider vinegar
- 1 tablespoon tamari or liquid aminos
- 1 tablespoon lemon juice
- 1 tablespoon gochujang
- 3 tablespoons sesame oil, divided
- 1 large clove garlic, finely minced (about 1 tablespoon)
- 1 head broccoli, cut into small florets
- 1 cup chopped kimchi
- 4 large organic eggs Freshly ground black pepper to taste

MAKE IT

Using cold water, rinse rice in a fine-mesh colander. In a medium pot, combine water, rice, and salt and bring to a boil. Lower the heat, cover, and simmer for another 35–40 minutes, or until all the liquid is absorbed and the rice is tender. If the liquid has cooked off but the rice is still firm, add a little more water and continue to cook on low.

Remove the rice from heat and let stand, covered, for 10 minutes.

Fill a large pot with water, add the vinegar, cover, and bring the mixture to a boil over high heat. Meanwhile, in a small bowl, whisk together the tamari, lemon juice, and gochujang until smooth. Set aside. Put 2 tablespoons oil in a large skillet over medium-high heat and warm until it just starts to shimmer. Add the garlic and stir for about 20 seconds. Add the broccoli, and toss it with the oil and garlic to coat. Continue to stir while cooking for another 4 minutes. Pour the tamari mixture over the broccoli and toss until the broccoli is coated. Cook another minute or 2 until the broccoli is tender. Divide the broccoli between shallow bowls for serving.

In the same skillet, heat the remaining oil over medium-high heat until it shimmers. Add the kimchi and stir until it's warmed through, about 3 minutes. Add the rice and toss to combine. Divide the rice between the bowls with the broccoli.

Once the water boils, reduce the heat to maintain a simmer. To cook the eggs, crack one into a small bowl and slowly pour it into the simmering water. Repeat with the remaining eggs. Cook until the whites are cooked through and firm but the yolks are still soft, about 3 minutes. Use a slotted spoon to remove the eggs, one at a time, and place one directly on the rice in each bowl. Sprinkle with salt and pepper.

Turmeric Cauliflower Cakes with Yogurt

SERVES 4

The active ingredient in turmeric, curcumin, has antioxidant and anti-inflammatory properties and helps lower cortisol, a stress hormone. And cauliflower is a nutritional powerhouse, one of the only vegetables to contain nearly every vitamin and mineral you need.

GATHER

- ¾ cup plain Greek yogurt, more for serving
- 2¼ teaspoons kosher salt, divided
- 1 teaspoon lemon juice
- 1 tablespoon turmeric powder, divided
- ⅛ teaspoon plus ¼ teaspoon freshly ground black pepper, divided
- 1½ pounds (approximately 4 heaping cups) cauliflower florets
- 2 large organic eggs
- ⅔ cup finely grated Parmesan cheese
- ⅓ cup panko
- 2 tablespoons minced shallot
- ⅛ teaspoon freshly grated nutmeg
- 2 tablespoons extra virgin olive oil, more as needed
  Store-bought pesto, for serving (optional)

MAKE IT

Line a rimmed baking tray with wax paper. In a small bowl, stir together the yogurt, ¼ teaspoon salt, lemon juice, 1 teaspoon turmeric powder, and ⅛ teaspoon pepper. Set aside.

Fill a large pot with water, the cauliflower, and 1 teaspoon salt, and bring to a boil over high heat.

Lower the heat and simmer for 10–12 minutes, or until the cauliflower can be easily pierced with a fork. Drain. Return the cauliflower to the pot and cook again over medium heat, stirring to remove any excess water.

Next, using a potato masher or the back of a spoon, mash the cauliflower until it's somewhat smooth, but a little texture remains. Stir in the remaining salt, 2 teaspoons turmeric powder, remaining pepper, eggs, cheese, panko, shallot, and nutmeg.

Using a ⅓-cup measure, form round patties and put them on the prepared baking tray.

Pour the oil in a medium skillet over medium-high heat, and heat until it just starts to shimmer.

Using a spatula, gently slide a few cakes into the skillet and fry for 3–4 minutes or until they start to turn golden brown. Don't flip them too soon or they will stick. Turn over and fry for another 3–4 minutes or until heated through. Transfer to a plate and repeat the process until all the cakes are cooked, adding more oil as needed.

Serve immediately topped with a dollop of yogurt or pesto.

Golden Cauliflower Falafel with Moringa-Tahini Drizzle

MAKES 16 PIECES

Common in India, moringa is a superfood that may be new to you. It's often called the "miracle tree" because it helps with so many ailments, ranging from protecting the liver to being antifungal, antiviral, and anti-inflammatory. Moringa is loaded with nutrition and has ten times the vitamin A of a carrot and fifteen times the iron of spinach. Yes, moringa is optional in this recipe, but it's something worth picking up at the health food store when you can.

GATHER
4	cups frozen riced cauliflower
¾	cup tahini, divided
⅔	cup almond flour
3 ½	teaspoons harissa seasoning, divided
1	teaspoon sea salt, divided
1	teaspoon moringa powder (optional)
1	bunch radishes

MAKE IT
Preheat oven to 350°F. Line a baking tray with parchment paper.

Defrost cauliflower, place in a towel, and squeeze out excess moisture.

Transfer to a bowl and add ½ cup tahini, almond flour, 3 teaspoons harissa seasoning, and ½ teaspoon sea salt.

Using 2 small tablespoons of mixture, form rounds and bake on lined baking tray for 15 minutes. Allow to cool for a few minutes before handling.

In a small bowl, mix remaining harissa seasoning, sea salt, moringa powder, if using, and remaining tahini until smooth.

Slice radishes and serve with cauliflower falafel and tahini drizzle.

Twice-Baked Sweet Potatoes with Jalapeño Yogurt, Avocado, and Pomegranate

SERVES 4

Here's a fun take on the traditional stuffed baked potato. Personally, I think sweet potatoes have more flavor, but opting for them is also healthier. Side by side, sweet potatoes have lower calories and carbs and also more fiber, vitamin A, and plenty of minerals.

GATHER

SWEET POTATOES

4	medium sweet potatoes
2	tablespoons olive oil, divided
½	teaspoon sea salt

JALAPEÑO YOGURT

4	jalapeños
1½	cups Greek yogurt
1	tablespoon olive oil
¾	teaspoon sea salt

AVOCADO-POMEGRANATE RELISH

1	small shallot
2	tablespoons apple cider vinegar
½	teaspoon sea salt
2	ripe avocados
½	cup pomegranate seeds
1	small bunch cilantro

MAKE IT

FOR THE POTATOES

Preheat oven to 425°F.

Tightly wrap each sweet potato in aluminum foil, place on a baking tray, and bake for 45–60 minutes, or until tender. While the potatoes bake, prepare the yogurt and relish.

FOR THE YOGURT

Place jalapeños over an open flame and blister for 2 minutes per side. Take off flame and place in a paper bag to steam for 10 minutes.

Remove and discard skins and stems, and cut into thin strips (optional: discard seeds for less spice).

Mix together the yogurt and olive oil in a bowl. Fold the jalapeño into the mixture and season with the salt. Refrigerate until ready to use.

FOR THE RELISH

Peel and chop shallot and place in a medium bowl along with vinegar and sea salt. Set mixture aside for 10 minutes to pickle shallots.

Dice avocados and fold into shallot mixture along with pomegranate seeds.

Remove stems from cilantro and chop leaves (⅓ cup). Fold into avocado-pomegranate relish and refrigerate until ready to serve.

When the potatoes are done, remove them from the oven. When cool enough to handle, unwrap, discard foil, and cut each potato in half lengthwise, or leave whole and cut a slit in the middle.

Scoop out majority of flesh into large bowl (approximately 2 cups). Fold in 1½ cups of jalapeño yogurt, reserving remainder for garnish.

Brush sweet potato skins with 1 tablespoon olive oil and return to tray. Overstuff with sweet potato mixture, drizzle with remaining olive oil, sprinkle with salt and bake on top rack for additional 15 minutes, or until the tops are golden.

Make indent in center of each potato, and spoon in ¼ cup of relish into each potato. Garnish with a dollop of reserved jalapeño yogurt.

Autumnal Nachos with Butternut Squash "Queso" and Walnut "Chorizo" Crumbles

SERVES 4

This is one of the top recipe requests from our companion TV show *Naturally, Danny Seo* on NBC. It's easy to see why: Ooey, gooey "cheese" sauce with "meaty" crumbles on top of crispy corn chips! Make this once and I promise you'll make it many more times. It's a winner.

GATHER

BUTTERNUT SQUASH "QUESO"

1	medium butternut squash
1	cup oat milk
¼	cup nutritional yeast
1	teaspoon chipotle powder
1	teaspoon sea salt
1	lime, zested and juiced

WALNUT "CHORIZO" CRUMBLES

1	cup walnuts
2	tablespoons avocado oil
1	tablespoon tomato paste
2	tablespoons Mexican seasoning
1	small bunch cilantro leaves, chopped
1	bag blue corn tortilla chips, for serving
1	lime, cut into wedges, for serving

MAKE IT

FOR THE "QUESO"

Preheat oven to 375°F. Line a baking tray with parchment paper.

Cut butternut squash in half lengthwise and remove seeds. Place squash, flesh side down, on prepared baking tray. Roast for 30 minutes, or until tender.

Remove tender squash flesh (approximately 3 cups) and add to a blender along with oat milk, nutritional yeast, chipotle powder, and salt. Process until smooth.

Stir lime zest and juice into butternut squash "queso" mixture.

FOR THE CRUMBLES

Chop walnuts coarsely and place in a bowl with hot water for 10 minutes to soften.

Drain and add to a small pan with avocado oil. Cook over medium heat for 2 minutes, stirring frequently. Reduce heat to low, add tomato paste and Mexican seasoning, cook for an additional minute, and remove from heat. Stir in cilantro leaves.

To serve, top tortilla chips with warm "queso" and walnut "chorizo" crumbles, with the lime wedges on the side.

Lentil-Walnut "Meat" Tacos

SERVES 4

This recipe hails from The Ranch Malibu, a health and wellness resort in Malibu, California. I spent a week there doing grueling hikes and workouts (and drinking plenty of water!) to find out what the big deal was about. Turns out, your whole mind and body get a massive reboot from just a one-week program. Part of that recharge is through food, and this recipe for their take on tacos is perhaps one of the tastiest meals I've ever had.

GATHER

TACO "MEAT"

1	cup dry brown lentils
2	cups filtered water
	Pinch of salt
2	cups walnuts, toasted
2	tablespoons cumin
2	tablespoons dried oregano
2	tablespoons onion powder
2	tablespoons garlic powder
2	teaspoons chipotle powder

TO SERVE

4	romaine or endive leaves or corn or gluten-free taco shells
	Vegan "cheddar" shreds
	Shredded red cabbage
	Cherry tomatoes, halved
	Scallions, thinly sliced
	Hot sauce

MAKE IT

Combine the lentils, water, and salt in a medium saucepan. Bring to a boil, then reduce heat to low and simmer for 15–20 minutes until the lentils are just soft. Remove from heat and drain any excess water. Set aside and allow to cool.

Then, to a food processor, add the lentils, walnuts, cumin, dried oregano, onion powder, and garlic powder, and pulse until it looks like ground taco meat. Over low heat, warm the "meat" in a skillet.

Assemble the tacos by placing the lentil "meat" mixture into lettuce leaves or a taco shell.

Top with "cheddar" shreds, shredded red cabbage, halved tomatoes, scallions, and your favorite hot sauce.

Kale Nests with Poached Eggs and Brown-Butter Croutons

SERVES 4

For the croutons, oil may be substituted for butter; either way they'll crisp up nicely. The key is to keep turning them. Fresher eggs poach better and older ones are best for hard boiling, since they peel more easily.

GATHER

KALE NESTS

1	bunch kale, stemmed and leaves torn into small pieces
2	teaspoons olive oil
½	teaspoon sea salt

BROWN-BUTTER CROUTONS

1½	cups (3 sticks) salted butter
1	small sourdough loaf, cut into small cubes

POACHED EGGS

1	tablespoon vinegar
8	organic eggs

MAKE IT

FOR THE KALE NESTS

Preheat oven to 350°F. Line a baking tray with parchment paper.

Toss the kale in olive oil and sea salt, and arrange in single layer on the prepared tray. Bake for 8–10 minutes, or until crisp.

FOR THE CROUTONS

In a large deep sauté pan, melt the butter and allow to cook for 1–2 minutes, or until golden. Add the bread cubes and stir frequently for 3–5 minutes, until they crisp up. Remove from heat and blot on paper towels.

FOR THE EGGS

Fill a small pot with water, coming ⅓ of the way up, and bring to a light simmer (temperature should range 160–180°F). Add the vinegar. Working in batches, carefully crack the eggs into the pot, cooking them for 2–3 minutes, or until the whites set and the yolks remain runny.

To serve, place crispy kale on serving plates or bowls. Carefully place 2 eggs in center. Garnish with brown-butter croutons.

Tandoori Coffee-Rubbed Roasted Sweet Potato Wedges with Cilantro-Cumin Yogurt

SERVES 2 TO 4

Yes, instant coffee. Because of the earthy, rich complex flavor coffee adds, using instant coffee takes the place of dried herbs in this recipe.

GATHER

SWEET POTATO WEDGES

2	large sweet potatoes, cut into wedges
1	tablespoon tandoori spice mix
1	tablespoon instant coffee
3	tablespoons olive oil
1	teaspoon sea salt

CILANTRO-CUMIN YOGURT

1	bunch cilantro
⅔	cup whole-milk yogurt
1	teaspoon ground cumin
1	clove garlic, minced
½	teaspoon sea salt
2	tablespoons olive oil

MAKE IT

FOR THE SWEET POTATO WEDGES

Preheat oven to 350°F. Line a baking tray with parchment paper.

Toss sweet potatoes wedges with spice mix, coffee, olive oil, and salt (omit or adjust amount if spice mix contains salt).

Spread into a single layer on lined baking tray and bake for 20 minutes. Gently toss and cook for an additional 15 minutes, or until crispy.

FOR THE YOGURT

Remove stems, chop cilantro (approximately ½ cup), and set aside. Add yogurt, cumin, garlic, and salt to a small bowl and stir until evenly combined. Gently swirl in ¼ cup of the cilantro and the olive oil.

Toss cooked sweet potatoes with remaining chopped cilantro and serve warm with the yogurt.

Coffee-Rubbed Portobello Fajitas

MAKES 6 FAJITAS

This is a great recipe to use up some vegetables in the fridge. Any type of mushroom will work in addition to carrots, potatoes, hearty greens, and green beans.

GATHER

PORTOBELLO FAJITAS

- 2 portobello mushrooms, cut into thick slices
- 8 miniature colorful bell peppers, halved and seeded
- 1 bunch scallions, bottoms cut into 1 inch pieces (reserve greens for future use)
- 3 tablespoons olive oil
- 2 espresso shots, or 3 ounces strong-brewed coffee
- 2 tablespoons fajita seasoning mix
- ½ teaspoon sea salt
- 6 medium whole-wheat or corn tortillas

AVOCADO "CREMA"

- ½ cup cashews, soaked in hot water for 15 minutes
- ½ cup filtered water
- 2 limes, zested and juiced
- 1 ripe avocado
- 1 teaspoon sea salt

MAKE IT

FOR THE FAJITAS

Preheat oven to 425°F.

Arrange mushrooms in a single layer in a cast iron skillet. Top with bell peppers and scallions.

In a small bowl, mix olive oil, coffee, fajita mix, and salt (omit if seasoning already contains salt) and pour evenly over vegetables.

Heat skillet over high heat until mixture bubbles. Transfer to top rack in oven and cook for 20 minutes, or until the vegetables are cooked through and marinade is reduced.

FOR THE AVOCADO "CREMA"

Drain and rinse soaked cashews. Add to blender with filtered water and process until cream forms. Add lime zest, lime juice, and avocado flesh and blend until smooth.

To serve, warm tortillas briefly in oven.

Spread a generous layer of avocado "crema" on each tortilla and top with mushrooms, peppers, and scallions.

Carrot Mash Tartine

SERVES 6

Rebecca French contributes this delicious open-faced sandwich—or tartine—idea. Rebecca says, "A few years back, a friend brought some savory squash toasts to our Thanksgiving feast. I swear, I ate four before the meal started. This carrot tartine is a riff on that recipe. The combination of carrot, coriander, and hazelnuts is divine, but the real key here is a good cheese."

GATHER

- 1 pound carrots (about 6 large carrots), peeled and cut into 1-inch rounds
- 1 tablespoon unsalted butter
- 2 teaspoons honey, more for drizzling
- ¼ teaspoon freshly ground coriander
- ¼ teaspoon kosher salt, more for seasoning Freshly ground black pepper to taste
- 6 to 8 pieces of whole-grain bread
- 1 teaspoon lemon juice
- 1 teaspoon extra virgin olive oil
- 1 cup pea shoots or other greens, such as arugula or watercress
- ½ cup ricotta cheese
- 3 tablespoons hazelnuts, chopped

MAKE IT

Place the carrots in a medium saucepan and bring to a boil. Lower the heat and simmer for 25–30 minutes, or until the rounds are fork-tender. Drain the carrots and return them to the saucepan. Add the butter, honey, coriander, salt, and pepper (a few good grinds on a pepper mill will do).

Mash the ingredients coarsely with a potato masher or large fork, incorporating everything together.

Meanwhile, toast the pieces of bread.

In a small bowl, whisk together the lemon juice and olive oil. Toss with the pea shoots or other greens and sprinkle with salt and pepper to taste.

To assemble the toasts, divide the ricotta among the pieces of toast (about a generous tablespoon on each) and spread evenly on each piece. Top with a thick layer of carrot mash and a small handful of greens. Sprinkle with hazelnuts and drizzle with a tiny bit of honey, if desired. Cut slices in half. Serve immediately.

SALAD FOR DINNER

Why not? Sometimes you just want a big salad with lots of veggies, grains, and a little protein for a meal. It's the kind of dinner that isn't just good for you, it also *feels* good. It's as if you know you're doing something nice for yourself, and it tastes really delicious, too.

This whole chapter has more than just side salads. We're talking hearty salads fit to be called entrées. I'm in love with the baked kale and falafel salad (page 80) because you can serve it as is or stuffed into a pita bread pocket. The grilled romaine (page 95) is a summertime game-changer, with the smokiness of the charring playing so well with the crisp leaves. And if you've never roasted radishes in your entire life, OMG, go to pages 84 or 92 right now. Even radish haters will flip for these soft and spicy little nuggets of pure deliciousness.

Red and White Quinoa Salad

SERVES 4

Versatile quinoa (a bulk bin favorite) has a delicate flavor that showcases whatever you put with it—in this case, toasted nuts and tangy cherries. You'll find that this surprising salad has a lot of texture but is still very light.

GATHER

½   cup red quinoa
½   cup white quinoa
1½   cups filtered water
¾   teaspoon salt, divided
½   cup dried cherries, chopped
½   cup blanched almonds, toasted
2   scallions, thinly sliced
½   cup extra virgin olive oil
¼   cup rice vinegar
2   tablespoons maple syrup

MAKE IT

Combine red quinoa, white quinoa, water, and ¼ teaspoon of salt in a 2-quart pot. Bring quinoa and water to boil. Reduce heat, cover pot, and simmer on lowest heat for 15–20 minutes.

Remove pot from heat and allow quinoa to steam, covered, another 10 minutes. Transfer quinoa to a bowl, fluff with fork, and cool to room temperature. Add cherries, almonds, and scallions.

Whisk together the oil, vinegar, syrup, and remaining salt. Toss salad with dressing.

Savory and Sweet Orzo with Olives, Raisins, and Onions

SERVES 8

Pair this simple dish with a red wine like a Pinot noir. It stands up to the strength of the olives and garlic without overpowering the sweetness of the raisins or the nutty character of the cheese.

GATHER

8	cups filtered water
1	tablespoon salt, plus ½ teaspoon, divided
2	cups orzo
3	tablespoons olive oil
1	onion, thinly sliced
3	cloves garlic, minced
½	cup pitted Kalamata olives, sliced
½	cup raisins, soaked in hot water for 10 minutes and drained
½	cup grated Reggiano Parmesan
¼	cup chopped parsley

MAKE IT

Bring 8 cups water to boil. Add 1 tablespoon salt.

Add orzo and boil until al dente, 8–10 minutes. Drain orzo and rinse with cold water.

In small sauté pan, heat oil over medium heat. Add onion and remaining salt. Sauté onion until caramelized, about 10 minutes. Add garlic and sauté 1 minute more.

Toss orzo with onion, garlic, olives, and raisins. Garnish each serving with Parmesan and parsley.

Cool and Crisp Salad with Baby Lentils

SERVES 4

This Middle Eastern-inspired salad packs in the protein so you can easily serve it as a lunch entrée or as a smaller first course. (Bonus: It also tastes amazing over seared or pan-fried tofu.)

GATHER

LENTIL SALAD

2	cups baby lentils
3 ½	cups filtered water
1	teaspoon salt
½	cup toasted pine nuts
¼	pound feta, crumbled
½	cucumber, diced
1	tomato, diced, or quartered cherry tomatoes
½	cup mint leaves, chopped

DRESSING

½	cup extra virgin olive oil
2	tablespoons maple syrup
½	teaspoon salt
¼	cup lemon juice
1	teaspoon mustard

MAKE IT

FOR THE LENTIL SALAD

Combine the lentils, water, and salt in a 2-quart pot. Bring to a simmer and cook, covered, until lentils are tender and all water is absorbed. Drain and cool to room temperature.

Toss the lentils with pine nuts, feta, cucumber, tomato, and mint.

FOR THE DRESSING

Whisk together the oil, syrup, salt, lemon juice, and mustard.

Toss the salad with the dressing before serving.

General Tso–Glazed Brussels Sprouts

SERVES 4

Many of the incredibly creative recipes you see in the pages of
Naturally, Danny Seo are the brainchild of our Culinary Director, Olivia
Roszkowski. For every issue, she is literally given a one sentence "theme"
to brainstorm with, and then she returns with a laundry list of no fewer
than 100 ideas. She's got a beautiful mind, and this is a beautifully
delicious use of healthy Brussels sprouts with a Chinese takeout twist.

GATHER

1	cup orange juice
2	tablespoons apple cider vinegar
¼	teaspoon red chili flakes
¾	teaspoon sea salt, divided
1	clove garlic, minced
1	tablespoon arrowroot starch
2	tablespoons sesame oil
1	pound Brussels sprouts, split lengthwise
⅓	cup filtered water
2	tablespoons black sesame seeds
2	scallions, sliced

MAKE IT

Add the orange juice, vinegar, chili flakes, ¼ teaspoon salt, garlic, and starch to a
small saucepan. Bring to a boil and allow mixture to thicken for 1 minute.

Add the sesame oil, Brussels sprouts, and remaining salt to a wok, or wide pan. Cook
for 3–5 minutes over high heat, or until sprouts are golden and crispy. Add the water
to create steam to soften sprouts, allowing it to evaporate. Fold in the sauce, and cook
until warmed through and the sauce has a glaze-like consistency.

Serve in a bowl, garnished with black sesame seeds and scallions.

Cranberry, Wild Rice, and Quinoa Salad

SERVES 8

Nicole Friday has been reinventing recipes for years, making family-friendly meals that are enlightened and lightened up with feel-good ingredients and a whole lot of love. This salad has the perfect combination of nutty wild rice, sweet cranberries, and protein-rich quinoa. Yes, it's perfect for Thanksgiving, but it's also a crowd-pleaser that will work anytime of the year.

GATHER

3	cups filtered water
¾	cup wild rice
½	cup red quinoa, rinsed
2	cups fresh cranberries
2	teaspoons, plus ¼ cup extra virgin olive oil
1	tablespoon granulated sugar
¼	cup raspberry vinegar
	Sea salt
	Freshly ground black pepper
2	stalks celery, diced medium
¾	cup diced aged goat cheese
½	cup chopped walnuts

MAKE IT

Bring water to a boil in a large saucepan. Add wild rice and cook for 30 minutes. Add quinoa to the rice, and cook until both are tender, about 15 minutes more. Drain and rinse with cold water until cool. Let stand.

Meanwhile, preheat oven to 400°F. Toss cranberries with 2 teaspoons oil and sugar. Roast in oven until slightly softened and caramelized, 10–15 minutes.

Whisk remaining oil, vinegar, and salt and pepper to taste in a large bowl. Add the rice and quinoa, celery, cheese, and walnuts and toss to combine. Gently mix in cranberries.

Chai-Glazed Beets with Crispy Seed Topping

SERVES 2 TO 4

Beets are the ultimate detoxifier for your blood and liver, so give yourself a second helping of this spicy and crunchy beet salad. By the way, if you get beet juice stains on your hands, just use a lemon to naturally remove the pigments. Cut the lemon in half and rub away to help fade the pinkish-red stains.

GATHER

CHAI-GLAZED BEETS

3   large beets, peeled and cut into wedges

1   (2-inch) piece ginger, cut into slices

10   cardamom pods

20   black peppercorns

10   whole cloves

3   cinnamon sticks

¼   teaspoon sea salt

1   tablespoon maple syrup

6   cups filtered water, or enough to cover beets

2   tablespoons lemon juice

CRISPY SEED TOPPING

2   tablespoons refined coconut oil

½   cup pumpkin seeds

¼   cup sunflower seeds

¼   cup black sesame seeds

    Sea salt to taste

MAKE IT

FOR THE BEETS

Place beets, ginger slices, cardamom pods, peppercorns, cloves, cinnamon sticks, salt, maple syrup, and water in a medium pot. (Optional: wrap spices in cheesecloth for easy removal.)

Bring beets to boil, reduce heat to low, and simmer for 30 minutes, or until beets are slightly tender. Do not overcook.

Remove beets, spices, and ginger slices and reduce beet cooking liquid for approximately 10 minutes, or until it has a syrup-like consistency.

Pour syrup and lemon juice over beets before serving, and toss gently.

FOR THE SEED TOPPING

Line a plate with a paper towel. Melt coconut oil in a medium sauté pan over medium heat for 30 seconds.

Add pumpkin and sunflower seeds and cook for 2 minutes, stirring frequently. Seeds will become golden and pop slightly.

Remove seeds from pan onto the plate to drain excess oil. Add in the black sesame seeds and sea salt, and stir to combine.

Garnish the beets with crispy seeds to serve.

Baked Kale Falafel with Creamy Tahini Dressing

MAKES 12 FALAFEL

Yes, baked not fried. It lightens up the Mediterranean classic and also helps keep the falafel moist. Be sure to add the warm falafel to the salad just before serving to prevent wilting the lettuce.

GATHER

BAKED KALE FALAFEL

2	tablespoons toasted sesame oil, more as needed
1	small red onion, chopped (approximately 1¼ cups)
1½	teaspoons sea salt
1½	teaspoons ground cumin
2	teaspoons dried dill
1	teaspoon garlic powder
1	small bunch kale, stemmed, steamed, and chopped, (approximately ½ cup)
1	(15-ounce) can chickpeas, drained and rinsed well
2	teaspoons lemon zest
2	teaspoons lemon juice
¼	cup breadcrumbs

TAHINI DRESSING

¼	cup tahini
2	tablespoons lemon juice
1	clove garlic, minced
1½	teaspoons maple syrup
½	teaspoon sea salt Pinch of red chili flakes
2	to 3 tablespoons filtered water
2	romaine hearts, chopped, for serving

MAKE IT

FOR THE BAKED KALE FALAFEL

Preheat oven to 350°F. Line a baking tray with parchment paper and grease with sesame oil.

Add sesame oil to a medium sauté pan over medium heat. Add the onion and salt and cook for 5 minutes, or until softened. Add the cumin, dill, and garlic powder and cook for additional 30 seconds. Remove from the heat and cool slightly.

In a medium bowl, add slightly cooled onion mixture, kale, chickpeas, lemon zest, and lemon juice. Use hands or wooden spoon to mash mixture until about half the chickpeas form a paste, while the other half remain visible in piece form. Fold in breadcrumbs to bind falafel mixture.

Scoop the falafel using a 2-tablespoon scoop, pressing it slightly between hands to form a uniform patty. Brush falafel tops with sesame oil and bake for 20–25 minutes, or until golden, flipping once halfway through cooking time.

FOR THE DRESSING

Whisk together the tahini, lemon juice, garlic, maple syrup, salt, chili flakes, and water (as needed) in a medium bowl until completely smooth.

To serve, place a bed of romaine on each serving plate. Top with warm falafel and then drizzle with tahini dressing.

Spring Panzanella with Radishes and Peas

SERVES 4 TO 6

Author and food blogger Anya Kassoff has been one of my favorite foodies to profile in the magazine. We spent the day with her and her photographer daughter back in 2018, and I literally may have licked the bowl clean after eating this salad. The crunchiness from the bread with the deep flavors from the garlic, radishes, and greens is a vegetable marriage made in heaven.

GATHER

VINAIGRETTE
- 4 tablespoons lemon juice
- 1 teaspoon Dijon mustard
- ¼ cup chopped fresh dill
- ¼ cup olive oil

PANZANELLA
- 4 slices whole-grain bread, torn or cut into cubes
- Olive oil, for drizzling
- 2 cloves garlic, minced
- Sea salt
- 1½ teaspoons neutral coconut oil
- 2 cups sugar snaps or snow peas, strings removed
- 2 cups fresh or frozen green English peas, thawed if frozen
- 10 to 15 radishes, thinly sliced
- 2 to 3 cups mesclun greens or other salad greens of choice
- Freshly ground black pepper
- Handful of pea shoots (optional)

MAKE IT

Preheat oven to 350°F. Line a rimmed baking tray with parchment paper.

In a medium bowl, combine the lemon juice, mustard, dill, and olive oil, and set aside.

Arrange the bread on the prepared baking tray, drizzle it with olive oil, and sprinkle with the garlic and salt to taste. Transfer to the oven and toast the bread for 20 minutes, until golden.

In the meantime, melt the coconut oil in a medium sauté pan over medium heat. Add the sugar snaps and a pinch of salt and sauté for 3–4 minutes, until they are bright green and lightly cooked, but still crispy. Add the peas and another pinch of salt, stir to coat for a minute, and then remove the pan from the heat.

Combine the toasted bread, cooked sugar snaps and peas, radishes, and greens in a large bowl. Pour the vinaigrette over top, season with freshly ground black pepper, and toss well. Scatter on the pea shoots, if using, and serve immediately.

Chili Honey–Roasted Radishes with Feta and Mint

SERVES 2 TO 4

In addition to being delicious, radishes are powerful liver detoxifiers. They contain a special antioxidant compound called RsPHGPx that can sweep out chemicals from pathways.

GATHER

- 2 bunches radishes (approximately 12), halved lengthwise
- 2 tablespoons olive oil
- ¼ teaspoon sea salt
- 1 tablespoon raw honey
  Pinch of red chili flakes
- ½ cup feta (approximately 2 ounces), crumbled
- 4 sprigs mint, stemmed

MAKE IT

Preheat oven to 350°F. Line a baking tray with parchment paper.

Toss radishes with olive oil and salt, and spread in a single layer, cut side down, on the prepared baking tray.

Bake for 10–15 minutes, or until the radishes have wilted lightly and have developed some color.

Add the honey to a small dish and fold in chili flakes. If mixture is too thick to drizzle, thin out with a teaspoon of water.

Plate radishes and drizzle with chili honey. Garnish dish with crumbled feta and mint.

Crunchy Spring Tabbouleh Salad

SERVES 4

Who knew cooked, fluffy quinoa could be transformed into something crispy and crunchy? It's also a great cooking technique to use on leftover quinoa the next day. If you can't find ras el hanout spice mix, just mix together equal parts paprika, coriander, ginger, and a pinch of saffron to make your own.

GATHER

TABBOULEH SALAD

3 cups cooked and refrigerated quinoa (1 cup uncooked quinoa)
1 teaspoon ras el hanout
1 bunch asparagus, blanched and cut diagonally into thirds
2 cups roughly chopped flat-leaf parsley leaves
1 cup roughly chopped mint leaves
4 scallions, thinly sliced
½ cup unsalted shelled pistachios, chopped
¼ cup dried currants
7 ounces feta, crumbled, for serving
Lemon wedges, for serving

DRESSING

2 tablespoons lemon juice
1 teaspoon pomegranate molasses
3 tablespoons extra virgin olive oil
Sea salt
Freshly ground black pepper

MAKE IT

Heat the broiler and set rack to upper third position. Spread 1 cup of the cooked and chilled quinoa on a baking sheet, sprinkle with the ras el hanout, and roast for 5 minutes, stirring and rotating the baking sheet occasionally. Roast for another 3 minutes until golden and crisp. Set aside.

To make the dressing, in a small bowl, mix the lemon juice, molasses, oil, salt, and pepper until well combined.

In a large bowl, add the remaining quinoa, asparagus, parsley, mint, scallions, pistachios, and currants and toss to combine. Add the dressing and gently toss. Top with crumbled feta and crunchy quinoa, and serve with lemon wedges.

Shaved Root Vegetable-Ribbon Salad with Cider-Poached Cranberries and Herbed Polenta Croutons

SERVES 4

Polenta croutons are a game changer. And that's what gives this simple salad a little more *oomph* to make it worthy of a dinnertime meal. Good to know: Rehydrating dried fruit in a vinegar, such as balsamic, will create balanced flavor notes of sweet and tart.

GATHER

VEGETABLE RIBBONS

4	scallions
3	medium rainbow carrots

CIDER-POACHED CRANBERRIES

1	cup dried cranberries
2	tablespoons apple cider vinegar
1	cup filtered water
½	teaspoon sea salt
2	tablespoons olive oil

HERBED POLENTA CROUTONS

1	cup polenta
3	cups filtered water
2	sprigs rosemary
3	tablespoons nutritional yeast
1	teaspoon sea salt
2	tablespoons olive oil

MAKE IT

FOR THE RIBBONS

Cut scallions into quarters lengthwise, and then cut into strips, discarding bottom roots. Place in cold water for 10 minutes to form ribbons.

Peel carrots. Use same vegetable peeler to shave carrots into thin ribbons and place in water with scallions for 10 minutes, or until ready to serve.

FOR THE CRANBERRIES

Add cranberries, vinegar, and water to a small pan. Bring to a simmer and cook for 10 minutes or until liquid is reduced. Take off heat, and stir in salt and oil.

FOR THE CROUTONS

Line a baking tray with parchment paper.

Add polenta to a medium pot and toast over medium heat for 2 minutes, stirring frequently. Add water, bring to a simmer, reduce heat, and cook for 10–15 minutes or until polenta is cooked through.

Remove stems and chop rosemary leaves (approximately 1 tablespoon). Stir into polenta mixture along with nutritional yeast and salt.

Spread warm polenta into a ½-inch-thick rectangle on prepared tray. Set in refrigerator for 15 minutes, and then cut into 1-inch squares.

Preheat a cast iron skillet over medium-high heat with olive oil. Crisp polenta squares for 2 minutes per side, or until golden.

To serve, drain the vegetables well and toss with cider-poached cranberries. Garnish with the croutons.

Peanut, Cilantro, and Purple Cabbage Rice-Paper Wraps

MAKES 6 WRAPS

Briefly boil the purple cabbage for the rice wraps to bring out its flavor and color—and to make it more digestible. To prevent rice paper from sticking to your hands, keep them wet and keep the others resting on a wet paper towel.

GATHER

⅓ cup crunchy peanut butter
3 tablespoons chili-garlic sauce, or to taste
1 lime, zested and juiced
2 teaspoons agave nectar
¾ teaspoon sea salt
1½ cups shredded purple cabbage
6 pieces rice paper
1 bunch cilantro

MAKE IT

Combine the peanut butter, chili-garlic sauce, lime zest, lime juice, agave, and salt in a bowl. Add a few tablespoons of water, if mixture is too thick.

Add cabbage to a sauté pan and cover with water. Bring to a boil and cook for 30 seconds to 1 minute to soften cabbage. Drain and rinse cabbage under cold water to cool.

Fill a shallow bowl with warm water. Rehydrate 1 piece of rice paper in water for 10–15 seconds, or until softened. Move to a plate to assemble.

Place cilantro, followed by cabbage, in an even row across the softened rice paper. Follow with a drizzle of peanut sauce and top with more cilantro.

Tuck in the sides of the rice paper, and roll away from you, keeping the filling intact. Repeat the process with the remaining ingredients.

Serve wraps with extra peanut sauce on the side.

Roasted Radishes with Turmeric Tahini

SERVES 4

Food blogger and cookbook author Anna Getty was featured in the Fall 2020 issue of the magazine. From her farm in Ojai, California, she whips up healthful takes using vegetables as the star and strong flavors to bring them to life. The great thing about radishes is you can get them year round in most places in the country. The yellow color of turmeric tahini adds a pop of color and a bright savory flavor.

GATHER

TURMERIC TAHINI DRESSING
- ¼ cup tahini
- 1 clove garlic, minced
- 1 lemon, juiced
- ¼ cup water
- ½ teaspoon salt, more as needed
- 1 teaspoon turmeric powder
- ⅛ teaspoon cayenne pepper (optional)
- ½ teaspoon maple syrup
- 2 tablespoons olive oil

ROASTED RADISHES
- 2 large bunches radishes, washed and leaves and tiny tails removed
- 3 tablespoons olive oil
- 3 teaspoons fresh thyme, minced, plus 4 to 5 sprigs thyme
  Salt to taste
  Freshly ground black pepper to taste
- ½ lemon, juiced

MAKE IT

FOR THE DRESSING
Place tahini, garlic, lemon juice, water, salt, turmeric powder, cayenne pepper, if using, and maple syrup in the bowl of a small food processor or into a blender and blend for 1–2 minutes. Keep the motor running and slowly add olive oil until blended. Adjust salt to taste. Transfer to a bowl and place in fridge while radishes are in the oven.

FOR THE RADISHES
Preheat oven to 400°F.

Cut the radishes in half and place them into a medium bowl. Add the olive oil, minced thyme, salt, and pepper, and mix well. Transfer to a medium baking dish. Place the fresh thyme sprigs around the dish.

Bake in the oven for 18–20 minutes, stirring once at the halfway point.

Remove the radishes from the oven and transfer to a serving dish. Sprinkle the lemon juice over the radishes and adjust the salt and pepper. Drizzle the turmeric tahini over the radishes, keeping the remaining tahini on the side in case you want more.

Grilled Romaine Salad with Maple-Dijon Dressing and Shaved Summer Corn

SERVES 2

If you think a plant-based BBQ is just frozen veggie burgers and potato salad, think again. This salad proves you can fire up the grill and make a salad in an entirely new way by charring the romaine hearts.

GATHER

MAPLE-DIJON DRESSING
½	cup Dijon mustard
2	tablespoons maple syrup
2	tablespoons almond butter
1	teaspoon sea salt
¼	cup olive oil

GRILLED ROMAINE SALAD
4	small romaine hearts
1	red onion, peeled and cut into ¼-inch rings
2	lemons, cut in half lengthwise and seeded
2	ears corn, husks removed

MAKE IT

FOR THE DRESSING
Mix together the mustard, syrup, almond butter, salt, and olive oil in a medium bowl.

FOR THE VEGETABLES
Preheat grill or grill pan.

Toss the romaine, onion, and lemon in Maple-Dijon Dressing and grill for 2 minutes per side, or until grill marks appear.

Place corn onto gas range or grill and blister for 2 minutes per side, or until slightly charred. Carefully use a sharp knife to shave off kernels from each ear of corn.

Squeeze grilled lemon over salad before enjoying. Serve with shaved corn.

Crunchy Mung Bean Sprout Salad

SERVES 6

Sprouting activates and multiplies the nutrients in mung beans, especially the B vitamins. Although sprouting beans takes a few days, it's minimal hands-on time, and it's so fun to watch the sprouts grow— like a science experiment. It's also very satisfying to eat the fruits (or sprouts) of your labor.

GATHER

DRESSING

2	tablespoons lemon juice
4	teaspoons tamari
½	teaspoon kosher salt
3	tablespoons extra virgin olive oil

MUNG BEAN SALAD

1	bunch red radishes (about 6), thinly sliced (about 1 cup)
2	large carrots, peeled and cut into 2-inch matchsticks (about 2 cups)
1	small jicama, peeled and cut into 2-inch matchsticks (about 2 cups)
2	cups packed mung bean sprouts or other crunchy sprouts
4	scallions, sliced, including the green parts (about ¼ cup)
⅓	cup fresh flat-leaf parsley leaves, chopped
¼	teaspoon kosher salt, more to taste
¼	teaspoon freshly ground black pepper

MAKE IT

FOR THE DRESSING

In a small bowl, whisk together the lemon juice, tamari, salt, and olive oil.

FOR THE SALAD

Combine radishes, carrots, jicama, mung bean sprouts, and scallions in a salad bowl.

Drizzle vegetables with the dressing and toss. Sprinkle with the parsley, salt, and pepper, and let the salad marinate.

Refrigerate for 1 hour or more before serving.

SOUP AS
A MEAL

Do you remember the Campbell's Soup advertising campaign where they proclaimed "It's soup that eats like a meal!" The idea was simple: a hearty bowl of soup can be plenty to eat for dinner.

I love making soups and stews from scratch because you can easily feed a crowd and adjust the recipe to accommodate whatever the group size might be. Plus, what's better than a bowl of soup and a sandwich? And in the case of the Quick Caramelized Spring Onion Soup (page 115), the bread bowl it's served in can be the delicious final treat at the end of the meal.

With the exception of fresh gazpachos, these recipes also do really well in the freezer. It's a great arsenal of recipes to have in the fall and winter months because you can make a large pot, enjoy it fresh, and then freeze the rest in portion-size amounts. When you don't have the time to make a dinner from scratch, just grab a portion of soup from the freezer.

Lastly, these recipes are versatile. I kinda think of it more like a GPS road map to the destination. Sure, you can follow step-by-step, but sometimes a little detour in ingredients can give you something even better. For example, if you have a few Parmesan cheese rinds in the fridge, toss them into the cauliflower chowder recipe (page 110)! Leftover sweet potatoes? Chop 'em up and throw them into the chili (page 119). It's all good.

Beach Soup

SERVES 6 TO 8

What a delicious way to get a ton of veggies into your diet (or your family's) that doesn't take a lot of time and effort. It's a crowd-pleaser and can accommodate almost anyone's dietary restrictions since it's totally plant-based, dairy-free, and gluten-free. Leftovers can be frozen and reheated later, too.

GATHER

- 2 cups broccoli or cauliflower florets
- 1 teaspoon plus 1 tablespoon rice bran oil, divided
- 1 leek, thinly sliced
- 2 cups small dice onions
- 2 cups small dice carrots
- 1 cup small dice celery
- 6 to 8 cups vegetable stock
- 1 bunch kale, stemmed and roughly chopped
- Salt to taste
- Freshly ground black pepper to taste
- White pepper to taste (optional)

MAKE IT

Preheat oven to 350°F. Line a baking tray with parchment paper.

Place the broccoli or cauliflower florets on prepared tray. Using 1 teaspoon of the oil, lightly oil and salt the vegetables. Roast for 15 minutes or until slightly charred. Set aside once finished.

While the broccoli or cauliflower is roasting, soak the leek in water for 15 minutes to remove any excess soil.

To a large pot over medium heat, add the remaining oil and sauté the leek and onions until tender. Next, add in the carrots and cook until tender. Finally, add the celery and salt to taste and cook until tender.

Once the vegetables are cooked, add the stock until desired consistency is reached and reduce heat to low.

Add the roasted broccoli or cauliflower florets. Add the chopped kale in any amount desired. Season with salt and freshly ground black pepper to taste. Season with white pepper, if using.

Cook until simmering and enjoy.

Tea-Steeped Caramelized Eggplant Pho

SERVES 4 TO 6

You read that right: tea-steeped pho! While this recipe calls for chai, you can use almost any tea you have in your pantry. Green, jasmine, and ginger tea are all great candidates to swap in; just remember to brew the tea on the strong side so the flavor really comes through.

GATHER

CARAMELIZED EGGPLANT
- 1 head garlic
- 1 large eggplant
- 3 tablespoons chili oil (or oil of choice and ½ teaspoon chili flakes)
- 2 tablespoons sesame seeds, more for garnish
- ¼ cup liquid aminos
- 2 tablespoons maple syrup

TEA BROTH
- ¼ cup loose chai tea
- 4 cups organic bone broth, or vegetable stock of choice
- 4 cups filtered water
- ¼ cup liquid aminos
- 1 (16-ounce) package wide rice noodles

GARNISH
- 1 bunch scallions
- 2 tablespoons chili oil, or to taste

MAKE IT

FOR THE EGGPLANT
Preheat oven to 375° F.

Cut garlic crosswise, press back together, wrap in foil and roast for 35 minutes.

Trim ends off eggplant and cut in half crosswise. Use spoon to scoop out and discard inner seeds. Cut into ½-inch-wide long strips.

Warm chili oil over high heat in medium to large Dutch oven.

Add eggplant and cook for 5–10 minutes, or until golden and slightly softened. Add sesame seeds, liquid aminos, and syrup and cook for additional few minutes until liquid is absorbed, stirring frequently. Remove eggplant and set aside.

Once garlic is roasted, squeeze it into Dutch oven and proceed to make broth.

FOR THE BROTH
Place tea in sachet, cheesecloth, or mesh tea ball.

Add broth to garlic in Dutch oven, along with filtered water and liquid aminos. Bring to a boil. Shut off heat and stir in noodles. Add tea sachet.

Steep for 15 minutes and remove tea sachet. Test noodles; if they are not tender, cook over high heat for additional few minutes.

FOR THE GARNISH
Cut scallions into strips. Place in cold water for a few minutes to crisp.

Pour broth into bowls and top with noodles, caramelized eggplant, scallions, and chili oil.

Autumnal Chickpea and Blistered Corn Chowder

SERVES 4 TO 6

There are two good reasons to blister and char corn on your cooktop or in your broiler: it brings out a new flavor dimension and it looks pretty cool, too. When you cook corn this way, its natural sugars caramelize.

GATHER

3 ears corn, husks removed

⅓ cup olive oil

3 (15.5-ounce) cans chickpeas (approximately 6 cups), drained and rinsed

2 red onions, diced (approximately 3 cups)

1 teaspoon sea salt

2 tablespoons Old Bay seasoning, more for garnish

3 tablespoons apple cider vinegar

4 cups vegetable stock

1 cup rolled oats

4 cups cold filtered water

4 scallions, sliced

MAKE IT

Place corn over open gas flame (alternatively broil corn in oven). Cook for 2 minutes per side or until blistered.

Cool slightly and use a sharp knife to shave corn kernels off cob (approximately 3 cups).

Heat medium to large Dutch oven over medium heat for 2 minutes. Add olive oil and chickpeas and cook for 5 minutes, stirring occasionally.

Stir in diced onions. Cook for 5 minutes or until onions soften, stirring occasionally. Fold in blistered corn, reserving ½ cup for garnish. Add salt, Old Bay seasoning, and vinegar and cook for additional minute. Add stock and bring to a simmer. Cook covered for 20 minutes.

Briefly rinse oats in colander. Add to blender along with filtered water. Blend for 20 seconds on high speed. Strain through fine mesh bag or cheesecloth.

Add oat "milk" to soup. Bring soup to a boil, stirring frequently for 2 minutes or until thickened.

Ladle hot soup into bowls. Top with reserved blistered corn, sliced scallions, and additional Old Bay seasoning.

Green Gazpacho with Pumpkin Seed Oil Drizzle

SERVES 4 TO 6

Did you know complex carbs, such as zucchini, green peas, cucumbers, and onions keep energy levels stable? Green yogurt, pumpkin seed oil, olive oil, and other healthy fats may help reduce inflammation, too. And did you know all of these ingredients are in this refreshingly cool gazpacho?

GATHER

- 2 cucumbers, seeded and cut into large chunks (about 3 cups)
- 1 small zucchini, cut into large chunks (about 1 heaping cup)
- 1 cup fresh or frozen shelled green peas, blanched
- ½ small yellow onion, coarsely chopped (about ¾ cup)
- 1 green bell pepper, seeded and cut into quarters
- 3 tablespoons lemon juice
- ¼ cup extra virgin olive oil
- 2 tablespoons white wine vinegar
- 1 teaspoon organic cane sugar
- 1 teaspoon kosher salt
- 1 clove garlic
- ¼ teaspoon ground coriander
- 1 teaspoon ground cumin
  Pinch of freshly ground white pepper
- 1 to 2 cups filtered water
  Plain Greek yogurt, for garnish
  Pumpkin seed oil, for garnish
  Freshly cut chives, for garnish

MAKE IT

Place the cucumbers, zucchini, peas, onion, bell pepper, lemon juice, olive oil, vinegar, sugar, salt, garlic, coriander, cumin, white pepper, and water in a blender. Process on low for 20 seconds, then turn to high and run until velvety smooth.

Chill for at least 2 hours.

Serve with a small dollop of plain Greek yogurt, a drizzle of pumpkin seed oil, and freshly cut chives.

Purple Plum and Shiso Gazpacho

SERVES 4

This dish gives a nod to Japanese cuisine by using ponzu sauce and shiso leaves. Shiso leaves are an herb common in Asia and they come from the mint family. If you can't find shiso leaves at your market, you can replace them with peppermint, lemon basil, or Thai basil to give this gazpacho its bright, herbal flavor. It's not quite the same as shiso, but it is very delicious.

GATHER

2	English cucumbers, peeled, seeded, and diced
1	jalapeño
3	cloves garlic
1	teaspoon sea salt
¼	cup yuzu juice (I like Eden Foods Ponzu Sauce)
8	large purple plums
¼	cup shiso leaves, for garnish

MAKE IT

Put cucumbers, jalapeño, and garlic into a medium bowl.

Toss vegetable mixture with salt and yuzu juice and allow to marinate at room temperature for 20 minutes.

Peel, pit, and rough chop plums, reserving any juices and add to cucumbers.

Reserve a few handfuls of vegetable mixture for garnish. Place the remaining mixture in a blender and blend until smooth. Note: if plums are not ripe, add a few teaspoons of agave nectar to taste.

Chill and serve gazpacho in bowls, topped with remaining vegetable mixture, and garnish with shiso leaves.

Creamy Cauliflower Chowder with Olive-Thyme Gremolata

SERVES 4

Talk about the perfect large pot of soup to make on a snowy day! This is a creamy dairy-free chowder. It's the oat flour that gives it that thick, creamy consistency. Good to know: when making the gremolata, avoid bitter undernotes by making sure to not use the pith of the lemon.

GATHER

CAULIFLOWER CHOWDER

3	tablespoons olive oil
1	medium onion, diced
2	teaspoons sea salt
1	medium cauliflower, cut into florets (approximately 6 cups)
3	cloves garlic, minced
¼	cup oat flour
¼	cup nutritional yeast
4	cups vegetable broth

ROASTED BABY GOLDEN POTATOES

1	pound baby golden potatoes, halved
2	tablespoons olive oil
1	teaspoon sea salt

OLIVE-THYME GREMOLATA

¼	cup pitted black olives
1	tablespoon olive oil
5	sprigs thyme
1	small clove garlic, minced
1	lemon, zested and juiced

MAKE IT

FOR THE CAULIFLOWER CHOWDER

Warm olive oil in a medium pot over medium heat. Add onion and salt and cook for 2 minutes, stirring occasionally. Add cauliflower florets and continue to cook for additional 5 minutes.

Add garlic, flour, and nutritional yeast and cook for additional minute. Add broth and bring mixture to a simmer. Cook, covered, for 20–25 minutes, or until cauliflower is tender. While the soup cooks, prepare the potatoes.

FOR THE POTATOES

Preheat oven to 375°F. Line a baking tray with parchment paper.

Toss potatoes with olive oil and salt. Spread into a single layer on prepared baking tray. Roast for 25 minutes, or until cooked through and golden.

FOR THE GREMOLATA

Rinse and chop olives coarsely and add to a small bowl with olive oil.

Remove stems from thyme for approximately 1 teaspoon leaves. Add to olive mixture, along with garlic and lemon juice and zest. Allow gremolata to marinate for at least 5 minutes before serving.

Serve chowder hot, garnished with roasted baby golden potatoes and olive-thyme gremolata.

Moroccan-Spiced Red Lentil Soup

SERVES 4

Don't be intimated by dried beans. Since lentils are so small, canned varieties tend to be clumpy and hard. In just 20 minutes, you can cook lentils from dried to tender, which makes this recipe a candidate for a fast and fresh favorite! By the way, if you're not familiar with harissa, you should be! It's a spicy Moroccan condiment made with ingredients ranging from roasted red peppers, chiles, and garlic, to preserved lemons, and saffron.

GATHER

2	tablespoons olive oil
1	yellow onion, diced
1	teaspoon sea salt
1	tablespoon harissa paste, more for garnish
¾	cup dried red lentils, rinsed
6	cups filtered water
6	sprigs cilantro, stemmed, and leaves chopped

MAKE IT

Warm olive oil in a medium pot over medium heat.

Add onion and salt and cook for 3–5 minutes, or until softened, stirring occasionally.

Stir in harissa paste and lentils until combined and cook for additional minute.

Add water to the lentil mixture, and bring to a simmer.

Reduce heat, and cook, covered, for 20 minutes, or until the lentils have softened.

Transfer soup to bowls and garnish with chopped cilantro.

Quick Caramelized Spring Onion Soup

SERVES 4

You have two ways to make this insanely delicious onion soup. One, you can follow the directions as is for soup that's light and perfectly seasoned. Or, you can do what I normally do: I throw in the bread I've hollowed out of the sourdough boules and use it to thicken the soup in the blender. Sure, it adds more carbs, but in my mind, who's counting?

GATHER

- ¼ cup avocado oil, divided
- 2 large yellow onions, sliced
- 1½ teaspoons sea salt, or to taste
- 1 bunch scallions, sliced, white and green parts divided
- ⅓ cup unsalted cashews
- 4 cups vegetable stock
- 4 small sourdough boules, hollowed out

MAKE IT

Warm 2 tablespoons of the avocado oil in a small pot over medium heat.

Add sliced onions and salt (adjust amount if using purchased stock containing salt), and stir to combine.

Stirring occasionally, cook for 8–10 minutes, or until onions have softened. Add sliced scallion whites and cashews, and cook for additional minute.

Add stock to onion mixture, reduce heat to low and simmer, covered, for 20 minutes.

While soup cooks, preheat oven to 375°F. Toast hollowed-out bread bowls on a baking tray for 3–5 minutes, or until crispy

In batches, transfer soup mixture to a high-speed blender and carefully blend until completely smooth. Season with additional salt, if desired.

Toss reserved sliced scallion greens (approximately ½ cup) with the remaining 2 tablespoons of avocado oil.

Pour soup into bread bowls and top with scallion greens mixture.

One-Pot Coffee-Chipotle Chili with Cornbread Dumplings

SERVES 4

You can make this chili without the dumplings, but I promise, it's worth the effort. The dumplings are versatile, too. You can add nutritional yeast, garlic powder, cayenne, or cilantro.

GATHER

COFFEE-CHIPOTLE CHILI

2	tablespoons olive oil
1	red onion, diced (approximately 1½ cups)
2	green bell peppers, seeded and diced (approximately 2½ cups)
2	teaspoons sea salt
2	teaspoons chipotle powder, or to taste
3	cups brewed coffee
1	tablespoon maple syrup
1	(15-ounce) can black beans, drained and rinsed

CORNBREAD DUMPLINGS

3	scallions, sliced (approximately ⅔ cup), divided
½	cup cornmeal
½	cup whole-wheat flour
½	teaspoon sea salt
½	teaspoon baking powder
½	cup coconut milk
1	ripe avocado, pitted, peeled, and mashed, for serving

MAKE IT

FOR THE CHILI

Heat oil in a pot over hight heat. Add onion, bell peppers, and salt. Cook for 4 minutes or until translucent.

Stir in chipotle powder, coffee, and syrup. Add beans, and simmer over low heat for 15 minutes.

FOR THE DUMPLINGS

Place half of the scallions in a large bowl, reserving remainder for garnish. Add cornmeal, flour, salt, baking powder, and milk to same bowl, mixing to create dough.

Form 16 tablespoon-size dumplings and gently lower into boiling chili. Cook for 6–8 minutes on high, or until dumplings are cooked through.

Divide dumplings among bowls, ladle in chili, and top with a dollop of avocado, and reserved scallions.

Detox Ramen with Mung Bean Noodles, Enokis, Tofu, and Lotus Root

SERVES 2

Kombu is dried sea kelp and is the star ingredient in making this ramen a detoxifying soup. It's been long believed that kombu can assist in detoxing heavy metals and chemicals out of the body and help support your overall immunity. It's earthy and salty flavor profile blends well with all the more neutral-tasting ingredients in this recipe.

GATHER

DETOX RAMEN

3	cups water
1	piece kombu
3	cloves garlic, sliced
1	bundle enoki mushrooms, bottoms trimmed
1	block firm tofu, cut into small cubes
1	medium lotus root, peeled and sliced
1	cup dried mung bean noodles, rehydrated

SEASONING

1	tablespoon sesame oil
2	tablespoons brown rice vinegar
3	tablespoons white miso paste
3	tablespoons ginger juice

MAKE IT

FOR THE RAMEN

Add water, kombu, and garlic to a small saucepan over medium heat, and bring to a gentle boil.

Add the enoki mushrooms, tofu, and lotus root slices, and simmer for 5–10 minutes, or until the vegetables have slightly softened. Add the rehydrated noodles and turn off heat.

FOR THE SEASONING

Season the ramen broth with sesame oil, vinegar, miso, and ginger juice, adjusting amounts to taste.

Transfer detox ramen to bowls and serve hot.

Black Bean and Sweet Potato Chili with Sliced Avocado

SERVES 2

If you're only going to whip up one recipe that can last a few days, this is the one. Eat it on its own. Top a baked sweet potato with it. Add a sprinkling of cheese and use it as dip. This one's got endless possibilities.

GATHER

2	tablespoons olive oil
1	onion, chopped
1	teaspoon sea salt
1	medium sweet potato, peeled and diced
2	cloves garlic, minced
1	jalapeño, chopped (optional)
1	tablespoon ground cumin
2	tablespoons chili powder
1	(15.5-ounce) can black beans, drained and rinsed
1	(14-ounce) can chopped tomatoes
4	cups vegetable stock
1	avocado, sliced, for garnish
	Fresh cilantro, for garnish
1	small bag blue corn tortilla chips, for serving

MAKE IT

In medium pot, heat oil over medium heat for 1 minute. Add the onion and salt and cook for 3–5 minutes, or until the onion pieces are softened and translucent, stirring occasionally.

Add the sweet potato and continue to cook for additional 3–5 minutes, stirring occasionally. Add the garlic, jalapeño to taste, if using, cumin, and chili powder and cook for 1 minute. Add the black beans, tomatoes, and vegetable stock.

Increase heat and bring to a simmer. Cook for 15–20 minutes or until sweet potatoes are softened.

Serve garnished with avocado slices and cilantro, with blue corn tortilla chips on the side.

Autumnal Ramen with Butternut Squash "Noodles," Ginger Bok Choy, and Miso-Scallion Broth

SERVES 4

I'm a minimalist when it comes to kitchen tools, but I do think a small spiralizer is a must-have. Buying pre-spiralized "noodles" may be a time-saver, but they are never really quite fresh enough to work in recipes like this; they can be slimy or crumble when cooked.

GATHER

GINGER BOK CHOY
2 tablespoons toasted
sesame oil
1 (1-inch) piece ginger,
peeled and minced
(approximately 2
tablespoons)
3 cloves garlic, minced
1 bunch bok
choy, chopped
(approximately 3 cups)
¼ teaspoon sea salt

BROTH AND "NOODLES"
6 scallions, sliced,
white and green
parts divided
2 pieces kombu
8 cups filtered water
1 small butternut
squash, seeded
and spiralized
(approximately 3 cups)
1 tablespoon
lemon juice
2 teaspoons sambal
red chili paste
¼ cup white miso
1 teaspoon sea salt

GARNISH
Reserved sliced
green scallion parts
1 sheet roasted nori,
cut into thin strips
1 tablespoon
sesame seeds
1 tablespoon toasted
sesame oil

MAKE IT

FOR THE BOK CHOY
Heat oil in a medium pot over medium heat.

Add ginger and garlic and cook for 1 minute, taking care not to brown. Add bok choy and salt and cook for additional minute, or until slightly wilted.

Distribute bok choy between serving bowls.

FOR THE BROTH AND "NOODLES"
In the same pot, add the sliced scallion whites, kombu, and water and bring to a simmer.

Add the squash and cook for 3 minutes, or until tender, taking care not to overcook. Using a slotted spoon, transfer "noodles" to serving bowls and discard kombu. Take broth off heat.

In a small bowl combine the lemon juice, chili paste, miso, and salt. If needed, use a small amount of broth to help form a uniform mixture. Stir liquid seasoning mixture into broth. Pour broth into bowls over "noodles" and greens.

TO SERVE
Garnish ramen bowls with sliced scallions, nori strips, sesame seeds, and a drizzle of toasted sesame oil.

Morning Miso Soup

SERVES 6

Having miso soup for breakfast is very common in Asian cultures. It's also really good for you as it's loaded with protein, B vitamins, dietary fiber, and helps boost your digestion, too.

Our take on miso soup is a bit more complicated than instant miso soup, but it's worth the extra effort. You can refrigerate the extra or portion it out in microwave safe bowls with lids. Just heat what you need and enjoy every morning!

GATHER

1 tablespoon neutral-flavored oil, such as canola or sesame

8 ounces shiitake mushrooms, stemmed, caps thinly sliced

6 cups filtered water

1 small piece kombu

4 tablespoons red miso

2 tablespoons white miso

1 tablespoon rice wine vinegar

1 tablespoon shoyu

4 ounces firm tofu, cut into small cubes

4 scallions, thinly sliced on an angle

4 ounces rice noodles, cooked according to package directions

MAKE IT

Heat the oil in a medium sauce pot over medium heat.

Add mushrooms and sauté until lightly browned, 4–5 minutes.

Add water and kombu. Bring to a boil and let simmer for 5–7 minutes.

Add red and white miso and whisk to dissolve. Season with vinegar and shoyu.

Add tofu, scallions, and cooked noodles, and heat through.

JUST PASTA

The deliciousness. The guilt. The quandary. Can pasta actually be good for you?

You betcha! Granted, coming to terms with portion size is something we all have to do—for every crave-worthy food—but these flavor-packed, veggie-forward recipes will leave you so satisfied that you'll feel both sated and proud of yourself when you reach the bottom of the bowl. What's the secret? Sauces crafted from nutrient-dense proteins mingling with vegetables that boost the fiber content help to fill you up and actually slow down the absorption of the carbohydrates in the pasta.

There are modern ideas that play on the idea of "pasta," too. Spiralizing sweet potatoes into a spaghetti shape gives it that mouth feel you love from pasta. And those shirataki noodles you see in the health food section of the supermarket that you've heard about but have no idea how to cook? We've got an idea on page 151 to transform them into something bright, filling, and—it's a miracle—nearly zero carbs.

Pecan Pesto with Spaghetti and Brussels Sprouts

SERVES 6

This dish is the perfect thing to serve to kids or anyone else claiming to dislike Brussels sprouts since a bunch of them are "hidden" in a delicious pesto.

GATHER

Sea salt

1 pound Brussels sprouts

½ cup toasted pecans or walnuts

1 clove garlic, minced

Leaves from 1 bunch parsley (about 1 cup, packed)

½ lemon, juiced

1 heaping tablespoon nutritional yeast (optional)

Freshly ground black pepper

½ cup olive oil

10 ounces spaghetti

MAKE IT

Bring a large pot of well-salted water to a boil.

Cut the tough ends off the Brussels sprouts and remove any discolored outer leaves. Cut the Brussels sprouts in half lengthwise (or in quarters, for large ones).

Blanch the Brussels sprouts in the boiling water for 5–8 minutes, until they are easily pierced with a fork but not mushy. Using a slotted spoon, transfer them from the pot into a colander. Rinse under cold water then set aside. Do not discard the blanching water.

Place the pecans or walnuts and garlic in a food processor and pulse the nuts into small pieces.

Add half of the blanched Brussels sprouts, parsley leaves, lemon juice, nutritional yeast, if using, salt, and pepper. Process until broken down into a chunky paste. With the motor still running, slowly pour in the olive oil and keep processing until well incorporated.

In the meantime, add the spaghetti to the pot with the Brussels sprout blanching water and cook until al dente. Drain the pasta, reserving ⅓ cup of the pasta water.

Add the drained pasta back to the pot, followed by the reserved Brussels sprouts, pesto, and the reserved pasta water. Toss until the spaghetti is evenly coated.

Soba Noodles with Roasted Grapes, Kale, and Sweet Potato

SERVES 4 TO 6

This dish tastes just as delicious cold as it does hot, if you manage to have any leftovers.

GATHER

Sea salt

3 packed cups Lacinato kale, cut into bite-size pieces

1 large sweet potato, peeled and cubed

10 ounces soba noodles

2 tablespoons neutral coconut oil or avocado oil

2 cups small, seedless purple, black, or red grapes

Splash of tamari

1 tablespoon toasted sesame oil

⅛ cup toasted sesame seeds, for garnish

MAKE IT

Bring a large pot of well-salted water to a boil. Add the kale and sweet potato to the pot and cook for 8–10 minutes, until the sweet potatoes are easily pierced with a fork but not mushy. Using a slotted spoon, transfer the vegetables to a colander or bowl.

Cook the noodles in the vegetable cooking water according to the instructions on the package. Drain the noodles, reserving ¼ cup of the cooking liquid. Briefly rinse the noodles under cold water.

While the noodles are cooking, warm the oil in a large skillet over medium-high heat. Add the grapes, along with a splash of tamari, and cook for 2–3 minutes, until most of the grapes burst.

Add the cooked kale and sweet potato to the skillet with the grapes, followed by the noodles and the reserved cooking liquid. Toss well to combine and drizzle the sesame oil over top. Toss again, until everything is coated and warmed through. Serve right away, garnished with the toasted sesame seeds.

Za'atar-Roasted Cauliflower and Chickpeas with Penne in Creamy Tahini Sauce

SERVES 6

Tahini is a paste made from sesame seeds and is one of the main ingredients in hummus. It's also one of the best plant-based sources of calcium out there.

GATHER

Sea salt

1 medium head of cauliflower, cut into florets

1½ cups cooked chickpeas

3 tablespoons olive oil or avocado oil, divided

1 tablespoon za'atar spice blend, more for serving

Freshly ground black pepper

1 bunch cilantro, leaves and stems torn

¼ cup sesame tahini

¼ cup lemon juice

2 cloves garlic, roughly chopped

1 teaspoon sriracha or other chili sauce of choice

¼ cup filtered water

10 ounces penne pasta

MAKE IT

Preheat oven to 400°F. Line a large baking tray with parchment paper. Set a large pot of well-salted water to boil for the penne.

On the baking tray, toss the cauliflower florets and chickpeas with 2 tablespoons of the oil, za'atar, and salt and pepper to taste, spreading everything out in a single layer. Roast for 25–30 minutes, or until the cauliflower florets are easily pierced with a fork and golden in places.

Reserve some cilantro leaves for garnish, if desired. Combine the torn cilantro, tahini, lemon juice, garlic, sriracha, remaining oil, and water in a blender. Blend into a smooth sauce.

In the meantime, cook the penne al dente in the prepared pot. Drain the penne and return it to the same pot.

Add the roasted cauliflower and chickpeas and pour the tahini sauce over top. Toss well, until everything is coated with the sauce. Serve right away, sprinkled with za'atar and garnished with the reserved cilantro leaves.

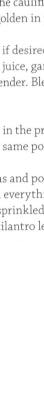

Coconut Turmeric Rice Noodles

SERVES 4 TO 6

If you happen to have fresh turmeric on hand, you can use it in place of turmeric powder for even more anti-inflammatory benefits. Use a 1-inch piece of fresh turmeric root, finely chopped, in place of the powder in this recipe.

GATHER

Sea salt
10 ounces rice noodles
2   tablespoons coconut oil
1   shallot, chopped
3   to 5 cloves garlic, minced
1   (½-inch) piece ginger, minced
1½ tablespoons ground turmeric
    Pinch of red chili flakes
1   tablespoon coconut sugar
    Splash of tamari
1   (13.5-ounce) can unsweetened Thai coconut milk
½   cup vegetable broth or purified water
½   cup toasted desiccated coconut and/or ½ cup toasted cashews, divided
    Cilantro leaves, for garnish (optional)

MAKE IT

Bring about 5 quarts of well-salted water to a boil. Remove the water from the heat, add the rice noodles, and soak them for 8–10 minutes, or according to the package instructions. Drain and rinse with cold water.

In the meantime, warm the coconut oil in a large saucepan over medium heat. Add the shallot, season with salt, and sauté for 5 minutes, until the shallot is soft. Add the garlic, ginger, turmeric, and red chili flakes and sauté for 2 more minutes.

Add the sugar, tamari, coconut milk, and broth or water, stir to combine, and simmer for 3 minutes.

Once drained, add the noodles to the pan with the sauce. Add about ⅔ of the toasted coconut and toss to coat. Serve right away, garnished with the rest of the coconut, cashews, and cilantro leaves, if using.

Butternut Squash, Parsnip, and Orzo Gratin

SERVES 6 TO 8

If you don't have a cast iron skillet, use a regular saucepan or frying pan to sauté the vegetables, then transfer them into a large, rimmed baking dish, mix with the rest of the ingredients, and proceed according to the recipe.

GATHER

1   small (or ½ large) butternut squash, peeled and seeded

1   large parsnip, peeled

2   tablespoons avocado oil or neutral coconut oil

1   large yellow onion, chopped
    Sea salt

3   to 5 cloves garlic, minced, divided

1   tablespoon tomato paste (optional)

2   tablespoons curry powder

10   ounces orzo

1   (13.5-ounce) can unsweetened Thai coconut milk

2½   cups vegetable broth

1   cup raw pumpkin seeds

1   heaping tablespoon nutritional yeast (optional)

MAKE IT

Preheat oven to 400°F. Shred the butternut squash and parsnip in a food processor fit with a shredding attachment and set aside. If necessary cut the squash into small pieces and quarter the parsnip lengthwise. Alternatively, you can shred everything by hand on a box grater.

Warm the oil in a 10-inch cast iron skillet over medium heat. Add the onion and a pinch of salt and sauté for 7 minutes, until translucent. Add about ⅔ of the garlic, tomato paste, if using, and curry powder, and stir to coat. Add the shredded vegetables and sauté for 2 minutes.

Add the orzo, coconut milk, broth, and a pinch of salt and stir to mix thoroughly. Cover the skillet, place in the oven, and bake for 30 minutes.

In the meantime, pulse the pumpkin seeds into small pieces, using a food processor with a regular blade attachment. Add the remaining garlic, a pinch of salt, and nutritional yeast, if using, and pulse to incorporate.

Take the skillet out of the oven when ready, remove the cover, and sprinkle the pumpkin seed mixture over top in an even layer. Bake the gratin, uncovered, for another 20 minutes. Remove from the oven and serve right away.

Penne and Acorn Squash with Parsnip Yogurt "Alfredo"

SERVES 4

The addition of nutmeg adds a spicy warmth that brings out the tangy notes of the protein-rich yogurt.

GATHER

ACORN SQUASH RINGS
1   acorn squash
1   small bunch sage
½   teaspoon sea salt
2   tablespoons olive oil, more for garnish

PARSNIP YOGURT "ALFREDO"
3   medium parsnips (approximately 1 pound)
1   pound organic penne pasta
1½   cups plain yogurt
¼   teaspoon ground nutmeg, more for garnish
3   cloves garlic
¼   cup nutritional yeast
2½   teaspoons sea salt, more for water
¼   teaspoon freshly ground black pepper, for garnish

MAKE IT

FOR THE RINGS
Preheat oven to 400°F. Line a baking tray with parchment paper. Set a large pot of well-salted water to boil.

Remove stems and seeds and slice acorn squash into ½-inch rings.

Remove stems from sage. Mince sage leaves (approximately 2 tablespoons) and toss with squash rings, salt, and olive oil.

Arrange squash rings in a single layer on the prepared tray and bake for 15 minutes or until golden and tender.

FOR THE "ALFREDO"
Peel and roughly chop parsnips. Add parsnips to a medium pot, fill halfway with water, and bring to a boil. Cook for 8–10 minutes, or until tender.

When the large pot of water begins to boil, cook the penne for 8–10 minutes, or as specified on the package, until slightly al dente.

Add yogurt, nutmeg, garlic, nutritional yeast, and salt to parsnips to a blender. Blend until smooth.

To serve, toss hot pasta with the sauce and garnish with acorn squash rings, additional nutmeg, ground pepper, and olive oil.

Quick Charcoal-Yogurt Pasta Dough with Herb Pesto

SERVES 4

This black pasta gets its color from activated charcoal, which you can find at a health food store. It's completely optional as it's more of a natural food coloring than a flavor additive. By the way, this dough is so versatile, too. Just roll it out into thin sheets and cut into fettuccine noodles to make a different variety.

GATHER

CHARCOAL-YOGURT PASTA DOUGH

- 2 cups sprouted wheat flour, more to dust surface
- 3 tablespoons activated charcoal (optional)
- 1¼ cups plain Greek yogurt
- 3 tablespoons sea salt

HERB PESTO

- 1 head broccoli
- 1 bunch chives, or other herbs (approximately 1 cup)
- 2 cloves garlic
- ½ cup grated pecorino cheese, more to garnish
- 1 teaspoon sea salt
- ⅓ cup olive oil, more for garnish
  Freshly ground pepper, for garnish

MAKE IT

FOR THE DOUGH

Place flour and charcoal, if using, in a food processor and pulse to distribute the charcoal. With the processor still running, start adding the yogurt by the tablespoon until a dough ball forms.

Remove the dough from the processor. Dust dough with flour, cover tightly with plastic wrap, and allow to rest for 20 minutes.

Cut dough into 8 sections and dust with flour. Roll each section into a 1-inch-wide log. Cut each log into ½-inch pieces. Use your thumb to press an indent into each pasta piece to form orecchiette.

Bring a large pot filled halfway with water to a boil. Add the salt and pasta and cook for 3–5 minutes, or until slightly al dente and the orecchiette floats to the top. Save pasta water to cook broccoli and herbs for pesto.

FOR THE PESTO

Cut broccoli into florets. Peel stalk and cut into rounds. Boil cut broccoli in pasta water for 2 minutes or until vibrant green and tender.

Dip chives or any bunch of leftover herbs, stems removed, into boiling water for 5 seconds. Place under cold running water to cool, squeeze out moisture, and chop into small pieces.

Add 1 ½ cups of broccoli florets to a food processor along with the chopped blanched herbs, garlic, pecorino, and salt. Process until smooth, streaming in the olive oil with the processor still running.

Spoon pesto onto each plate and top with broccoli stalks, orecchiette, and broccoli florets. Dollop with additional pesto and garnish with a drizzle of olive oil, pecorino, and freshly ground black pepper.

Golden Carrot "Spaghetti" with Molten Kale "Cream"

SERVES 2

Root vegetables such as carrots work well spiralized because of their firmer flesh and lower water content. Nutritional yeast not only lends cheesiness, but also does a fabulous job thickening the sauce.

GATHER

CARROT "SPAGHETTI"
4   large golden or white carrots
¼   teaspoon sea salt

KALE CRISPS
1   small bunch curly kale
1   tablespoon olive oil
¼   teaspoon sea salt

MOLTEN KALE "CREAM"
3   cups oat milk
¼   cup agar agar flakes (or ½ cup of cornstarch)
¼   cup nutritional yeast, more for garnish
1   teaspoon sea salt
2   cloves garlic
     Olive oil, for serving
     Freshly ground black pepper, for serving
     Red chili flakes, for serving

MAKE IT

FOR THE "SPAGHETTI"
Peel carrots and cut into long, thin strips lengthwise. Alternatively pass through a spiralizer.

Massage carrot "spaghetti" with sea salt for about 30 seconds, or until tenderized.

FOR THE CRISPS
Preheat oven to 300°F. Line a baking tray with parchment paper.

Remove stems from kale and tear leaves into small pieces. Massage with olive oil and salt for 1 minute, or until tender and vibrant green.

Spread the kale onto the prepared tray and bake for 15 minutes or until lightly crispy.

FOR THE "CREAM"
Add milk, agar agar flakes, nutritional yeast, and salt to a small pot. Bring to a simmer over medium heat, and cook for 3–5 minutes, or until agar dissolves and mixture slightly thickens.

Add mixture along with kale crisps (approximately 2 cups) and garlic to a blender and process until kale is broken up into small pieces. Toss molten "cream" with carrot "spaghetti."

Plate "spaghetti," and garnish with nutritional yeast, a drizzle of olive oil, pepper, and chili flakes. Serve warm.

Stovetop Winter Greens and Tofu "Ricotta" Lasagna Rolls

SERVES 4

You can serve this dish with your favorite pasta sauce. For a quick bean "ragu" sauce, blend together canned white beans with rosemary, garlic, and vegetable stock. Simply bring to a simmer and serve it up. Also, when in a pinch, you can substitute frozen greens.

GATHER
- 1 (1-pound) package lasagna noodles
- 6 tablespoons olive oil, divided, more to grease pan and toss noodles
- 2 bunches Lacinato kale, stemmed and chopped
- 6 shallots, sliced
- 1 cup sun-dried tomatoes, cut into thick strips
- 5 teaspoons sea salt, divided
- 2 blocks firm tofu, divided
- ½ cup filtered water
- 4 cloves garlic
- 3 sprigs rosemary, stemmed
- 2 lemons, zested and juiced

MAKE IT
Preheat oven to 450°F.

Bring water to a boil in a large pot. Cook lasagna noodles for 8 minutes, or until cooked through. Strain and cool with cold running water to prevent sticking and toss with olive oil.

Place kale in a large bowl and massage for a few minutes until tender.

Warm 3 tablespoons of olive oil in large pan over medium heat. Add shallots, tomatoes, and 1½ teaspoons salt and cook for 5 minutes, or until tender. Fold into massaged kale.

Squeeze liquid out of tofu with hands over a strainer. In a blender, process half of the tofu, remaining salt, remaining olive oil, water, garlic, rosemary, and lemon zest and juice, until smooth. Crumble and fold in remaining tofu.

Grease baking dish with olive oil. Top each lasagna noodle with the "ricotta" mixture, kale and tomato mixture, roll, and arrange in dish. Repeat with remaining noodles.

Cover and bake for 10 minutes or until heated through.

Grilled Zucchini "Ravioli" with Pumpkin-Cashew "Ricotta"

SERVES 4

This recipe came from Elizabeth Stein, founder of the natural foods company Purely Elizabeth. She says the pumpkin-cashew "ricotta" is incredibly versatile and can be used in lasagna, too. This recipe also swaps out sheets of pasta for zucchini for those looking for a low-carb alternative.

GATHER
- 2 zucchini
- 1 tablespoon olive oil, more for zucchini
- 1 teaspoon salt, more for zucchini
  Freshly ground black pepper
- ½ cup walnuts, chopped
- 2 cups raw cashews
- 1 (15-ounce) can pumpkin purée
- 1 clove garlic
- 1 lemon, juiced
- 1 pint cherry tomatoes

MAKE IT
Preheat a grill to medium-high heat.

Slice the zucchini lengthwise into thin ⅛-inch slices using a mandolin slicer or vegetable peeler. Transfer slices to a large bowl and toss with olive oil, salt, and pepper to coat.

Lay the slices of zucchini out over the grates and grill until light char marks are visible. Flip the zucchini over and cook until the other side is charred as well. Remove the grilled zucchini from the grill and place on a plate to cool.

To make the "ricotta", use a high-speed blender and add walnuts, cashews, pumpkin, garlic, lemon juice, and 1 teaspoon salt and blend until smooth. Add water as needed if the mixture is too thick.

Preheat oven to 350°F.

Add the cherry tomatoes to a cast iron skillet, covering the bottom of the skillet. Drizzle with 1 tablespoon of olive oil.

Once the zucchini slices have cooled to the touch, place 1 tablespoon of the "ricotta" at the end of each zucchini slice and roll. Place on top of the cherry tomatoes. Repeat the process with the remaining zucchini slices.

Place the skillet in the oven and bake for 25 minutes or until tomatoes are warm and soft and the ricotta is warm.

Lentil "Bolognese" with Marinated Cherry Tomatoes

SERVES 4

A traditional Bolognese sauce is meat-based and usually made with ground beef. This vegetarian version uses lentils for the "meat," which makes it a plant-based, protein-packed sauce that satisfies without the guilt.

GATHER

BOLOGNESE

- 1 cup dried black lentils, rinsed (or 3 cups cooked lentils)
- 8 cups filtered water
- ⅓ cup olive oil
- 2 medium red onions, diced (approximately 3 cups)
- 2 cups (4 ounces) shiitake mushrooms, stemmed and tops roughly chopped
- 2 teaspoons sea salt
- 4 cloves garlic, minced
- 1 (5-ounce) container baby spinach
- 1 (1-pound) package rigatoni

MARINATED CHERRY TOMATOES

- 2 pints cherry tomatoes
- ¼ cup olive oil
- 2 teaspoons sea salt
- ½ cup white wine vinegar
- ¼ teaspoon red chili flakes, more for garnish

MAKE IT

FOR THE BOLOGNESE

Add the lentils to a medium to large Dutch oven. Add the water. Cover and bring to a simmer. Cook for 25–30 minutes, or until tender. Strain and gently rinse lentils until water runs clear. Set aside.

Rinse the Dutch oven and set over high heat. Add the olive oil. Add onions, shiitakes, and salt. Cook for 5 minutes, stirring occasionally. Add garlic and cooked lentils and cook for additional 5 minutes. Turn off heat and fold in baby spinach. Transfer mixture to a bowl.

Rinse and fill Dutch oven three-quarters full with water. Bring to a boil and cook rigatoni for according to the package instructions.

Strain pasta, return to pot, and gently toss with "Bolognese" mixture.

FOR THE TOMATOES

Meanwhile, prepare the tomatoes. Cut tomatoes in half.

Place Dutch oven or sauté pan over high heat. Add cherry tomatoes, olive oil, salt, vinegar, and chili flakes. Cook for 3 minutes or until tomatoes have slightly softened.

To serve, top the pasta "Bolognese" with the marinated tomatoes. Garnish with additional chili flakes.

Cold Sesame-Peanut "Zoodles"

SERVES 2

This is a fast and super easy recipe that literally takes minutes to make. I like to think of it more as a "pasta" salad to go with a main dish, but it's great on its own. Good to know: Massaging the zucchini slices with salt will soften them, making them more noodle-like.

GATHER

3	medium zucchini
1	small purple cabbage
½	cup roasted peanuts
3	tablespoons toasted sesame chili oil
2	tablespoons rice vinegar
2	teaspoons maple syrup
3	tablespoons tamari

MAKE IT

Spiralize zucchinis on a large blade and place in large bowl.

Thinly slice cabbage (approximately 1 cup) and place in same bowl.

Chop peanuts and toss with vegetables.

Whisk together oil, vinegar, syrup, and tamari and pour over vegetables. Toss to combine.

Shirataki Noodles with Macadamia "Ricotta," Broccoli, and Mint

SERVES 2

This Japanese noodle is made from the starch of konjac "yams," and they are often referred to as "miracle pasta" because they are low in carbohydrates and have virtually no calories. This recipe is keto-friendly and uses coconut oil as a good fat to help you feel full and satiated.

GATHER
- ¾ cup macadamia nuts
- 2 tablespoons refined coconut oil
- 1 tablespoon umeboshi paste
- 1 clove garlic
- 1 small head broccoli
- 1 (8-ounce) package shirataki noodles
- 1 small bunch mint

MAKE IT
Bring a medium pot of water to a boil.

Add macadamia nuts to water and cook for 1 minute or until softened.

Transfer nuts to food processor along with coconut oil, umeboshi paste, garlic, and ¼ cup of the hot water and process for 30 seconds, or until mixture resembles ricotta but is not completely smooth.

Cut broccoli into florets. Drain and rinse shirataki noodles well.

Add shirataki noodles to boiling water and cook for 2 minutes. Add broccoli and cook for 30 seconds longer. Drain and plate. Garnish with dollops of macadamia "ricotta" and fresh mint leaves.

Zucchini "Pappardelle" with Avocado-Basil "Alfredo"

SERVES 2

So you might be asking, another zucchini "pasta" alternative recipe? Yes, and here's why: if it's summer, there is a bumper crop of zucchini. And you'll want to have another delicious way to serve it up. This one is full of good fats, and it's creamy, bright, and fresh.

GATHER
- 3 medium zucchini
- 1 teaspoon sea salt, divided
- 1 packed cup fresh basil leaves, more for garnish
- 1 ripe avocado
- 2 cloves garlic
- ¼ cup avocado oil, more for garnish
- 1 lemon, juiced (approximately 3 tablespoons)
- ¼ cup filtered water

MAKE IT
Line a plate with paper towels. Slice zucchini lengthwise into thin slices. Cut into wide ½-inch strips, and set on plate. Sprinkle with ½ teaspoon salt, and let sit for 10 minutes. Squeeze out excess moisture.

In the meantime, make the "alfredo" sauce. Add basil to a blender, along with remaining salt, avocado, garlic, avocado oil, lemon juice, and water. Blend until smooth.

Plate zucchini strips and garnish with dollops of avocado "alfredo," extra basil, and a drizzle of avocado oil.

Mochi Gnocchi with Shimeji Mushrooms and Snap Peas

SERVES 2

Making Japanese food at home can be intimidating. It's understandable—Japanese cuisine is artful. But it doesn't mean you have to be a sushi master or ramen wizard to create dishes steeped in the flavors of Japan. Here, a few simple seasonal ingredients help transform mochi into a savory unexpected meal. We like to use Eden Foods Sprouted Brown Rice Mochi in this recipe.

GATHER

½ teaspoon sea salt, more for boiling water
6 glutinous rice cake blocks (mochi)
3 tablespoons toasted sesame oil
1 cup snap peas, strings removed and cut in half lengthwise
1 bunch shimeji mushrooms, tough bottoms removed
3 cloves garlic, sliced
1 jalapeño, minced

MAKE IT

Bring a medium pot of water to a boil and season with a generous sprinkling of salt.

Cut rice cake blocks into small ½-inch squares and, working in batches, drop into boiling water. Cook for 90 seconds and transfer to plates.

Warm sesame oil in a large pan over medium heat and add snap peas and mushrooms. Cook for 3–5 minutes. Season with ½ teaspoon salt.

Add garlic and jalapeño and cook for additional minute.

Top mochi gnocchi with vegetables and serve warm.

Summer Linguine with Poppy Seeds, Zucchini Ribbons, and Pansies in Lemon-Almond "Alfredo"

SERVES 2

This recipe calls for edible flowers, but don't skip it if you can't find any. It's the addition of the yellow bell pepper, lemon juice, and nutritional yeast in the dairy-free "Alfredo" sauce that makes this a bright, summertime favorite. Enjoy it hot or cold!

GATHER

LEMON-ALMOND "ALFREDO"

- 1 yellow bell pepper, ribs removed, seeded, and diced
- 1 tablespoon lemon zest
- ¼ cup lemon juice
- ⅓ cup almond butter
- ¼ cup nutritional yeast
- 1 teaspoon black pepper
- 2 teaspoons sea salt, or to taste
- 1 teaspoon lemon extract

SUMMER LINGUINE

- ½ pound whole-wheat linguine
- 2 zucchini, cut into ribbons with peeler
- 1 teaspoon sea salt, or to taste
  Pinch of red chili flakes
- 2 tablespoons poppy seeds
- 12 pansies, or edible flower of choice (optional)

MAKE IT

FOR THE "ALFREDO"

Add bell pepper, lemon zest, lemon juice, almond butter, nutritional yeast, pepper, salt, and lemon extract to a high-speed blender.

Process on high speed until smooth, and set aside. (Note: mixture will taste concentrated and slightly salty before tossed with pasta.)

FOR THE LINGUINE

Bring a medium pot filled halfway with water to a rolling boil.

Add the linguine and cook for 6 minutes or until tender, taking care not to overcook. Carefully drain pasta and toss with zucchini ribbons, salt, chili flakes, and Lemon Almond "Alfredo." If desired, mixture can be thinned slightly with small amount of pasta water.

Plate pasta and garnish with poppy seeds and edible flowers, if using.

Turmeric Gnocchi with Purple Asparagus and Pan-fried Greens

SERVES 4

Feel free to substitute any greens you might have on hand, such as kale, collards, radicchio, or baby spinach. Good to know: Shallots are less pungent than onions or garlic, so they won't overpower this dish. The petite powerhouses are also rich in antioxidants, minerals, and vitamins.

GATHER

GNOCCHI

1 medium sweet potato, baked until tender, peeled, and mashed (approximately 1 cup)
1 organic egg
2 teaspoons sea salt
1 cup whole-wheat flour
1 teaspoon turmeric powder

PAN-FRIED GREENS

2 tablespoons olive oil
2 medium shallots, sliced (approximately ¾ cup)
1 teaspoon sea salt
1 bunch purple asparagus, trimmed, and cut into 1-inch pieces (about 2 cups)
1 bunch chard, stemmed and leaves roughly chopped (about 4 cups)
1 teaspoon poppy seeds

MAKE IT

FOR THE GNOCCHI

Fill a medium pot halfway with water and bring to a boil.

In a medium bowl, gently mix together the cooked sweet potato, egg, salt, flour, and turmeric powder until a dough forms.

Take a quarter of the dough, and roll into an approximately ½-inch-thick log. Cut dough into 1-inch rectangles, drop into boiling water, and cook for 3–5 minutes or until the gnocchi start to float.

Remove cooked gnocchi from water and set aside. Repeat with remaining gnocchi dough.

FOR THE PAN-FRIED GREENS

Warm olive oil in a large sauté pan over medium heat.

Add shallots and salt and cook for 2 minutes, or until translucent. Add asparagus and cook for additional minute.

Stir in cooked gnocchi and chard, cover with lid, and cook for 1 minute or until the greens are wilted.

Plate and garnish with poppy seeds.

Spiralized Sweet Potato Noodles with Sage Pesto

SERVES 4

This was one of the most popular recipes from my NBC TV show *Naturally, Danny Seo*. You'll know why when you have the first bite of this sweet, savory, salty, nutty dish. It's the perfect representative of "umami," which is the science of finding that perfect combination that creates a pleasant savory taste.

GATHER

1	tablespoon sea salt
1	pound sweet potatoes, peeled
1	tablespoon, plus ⅓ cup olive oil, divided
¾	cup pecans, toasted
¼	cup sage leaves
¾	cup parsley
1	clove garlic
2	tablespoons miso

MAKE IT

Bring a medium pot filled halfway with water to a boil and season with the salt.

Use a spiralizer to turn the sweet potatoes into "noodles" (alternatively use a peeler to create more broad noodles).

Cook sweet potatoes for 2–5 minutes, or just until tender, taking care not to overcook. Drain and toss with 1 tablespoon of olive oil.

In a food processor, pulse the pecans lightly. Add the sage, parsley, garlic, and miso and process until smooth. With the processor still running, slowly stream in the remaining olive oil.

To serve, fold in the pesto with sweet potato noodles.

ALMOST ONE-POT WONDERS

If the actual clean-up is what you dread most about cooking, this chapter is for you. We're talking about a bare number of pots, pans, skillets, and baking trays getting dirty here. In fact, sometimes we're talking about just one.

When I looked back at the archives of the magazine, I noticed a trend. Over time, the recipes were getting more streamlined to keep clean-up to a minimum. Is it any surprise? It doesn't matter what time of the year it is, with cool weather and dark evenings, we want to get a hot meal on the table as soon as possible, and with warm air and long days, we still want to get dinner on the outside table quickly so we can enjoy our summer nights. It's fast-food, but done right.

Other than dirtying up a few pans or pots, you'll find some clever tips and hacks here. These recipes are also easy to double for a party; all you have to do is find a larger cooking vessel to get the same great results. And don't forget dessert: ice cream scooped into one bowl also makes for a one-pot (or bowl) wonder, too.

Almond Milk-Creamed Corn Pudding with Blistered Shishitos

SERVES 4 TO 6

Don't have almond milk? You can also blend ¼ cup of almond butter with 1½ cups of water to make your own in a pinch.

GATHER

WET INGREDIENTS

¼	cup refined coconut oil
1	medium yellow onion, diced
2	tablespoons Hatch chiles
4	ears corn, husks removed
2	tablespoons apple cider vinegar
1½	cups almond milk

DRY INGREDIENTS

¼	cup nutritional yeast
1	teaspoon sea salt
1	teaspoon garlic powder
1	cup fine cornmeal
1	teaspoon baking powder
¼	teaspoon cayenne pepper

BLISTERED SHISHITOS

12	shishito peppers
2	tablespoons olive oil
¼	teaspoon sea salt

MAKE IT

FOR THE WET AND DRY INGREDIENTS

Preheat oven to 350°F.

Add the coconut oil to a medium cast iron skillet and sauté diced onion over medium heat. Add chiles. Set aside to cool.

Blister corn over stovetop gas flame for 30 seconds per side, or until lightly charred (or place under oven broiler for 2–3 minutes). Cut kernels from ears of corn.

In a blender, put half of onion mixture, corn, vinegar, and almond milk. Add the nutritional yeast, salt, garlic powder, cornmeal, baking powder, and cayenne. Blend until smooth.

Fold in remaining onion with corn and transfer to the same cast iron skillet.

Bake for 40 minutes, or until pudding is lightly set. Cool for 10 minutes before slicing; cool completely for perfect slices.

FOR THE SHISHITOS

While the pudding cools, prepare the shishitos. Toss shishitos with olive oil and salt.

Preheat a sauté or grill pan over high heat until almost smoking and carefully add the peppers. Cook for 30 seconds to 1 minute, turning frequently.

Garnish the pudding with the shishitos.

Balsamic Beet and Pumpkin Seed "Ricotta" Risotto

SERVES 4 TO 6

Yes, the "ricotta" in this recipe is in quotes for good reason, it's made from tofu! This delicious nondairy "cheese" is packed with protein and just as good as the real thing.

GATHER

PUMPKIN SEED "RICOTTA"

1	cup shelled pumpkin seeds
4	cloves garlic, smashed
2	tablespoons olive oil
½	block firm tofu, rinsed, crumbled, and excess water removed
1	lemon, zested and juiced
2	tablespoons white miso
1	teaspoon sea salt

BALSAMIC BEETS

2	red beets, peeled and cut into bite-size pieces
2	tablespoons balsamic vinegar
2	tablespoons olive oil
2	teaspoons sea salt

RISOTTO

3	shallots, diced (approximately 1¼ cups)
¼	cup white wine vinegar
2	tablespoons olive oil
2	teaspoons sea salt
2	tablespoons white miso
2	cups jasmine rice
4	cups organic bone broth, or stock of choice
1	cup baby arugula, or greens of choice

MAKE IT

FOR THE "RICOTTA"

Add pumpkin seeds to a medium to large Dutch oven. Cook over medium heat for 2 minutes, or until they start to pop.

Transfer ¾ cup pumpkin seeds into food processor, reserving remaining ¼ cup for garnish. Pulse into a powder.

Add the garlic and olive oil to the Dutch oven over medium heat. Sizzle briefly until fragrant.

Add garlic mixture, tofu, lemon zest, lemon juice, miso, and salt to the food processor. Process until thick and smooth, adding a splash of water if mixture is too thick. Refrigerate until needed.

FOR THE BEETS

Preheat oven to 400°F and line a baking tray with parchment paper.

Arrange beets in a pile on the middle of the parchment paper. Drizzle with vinegar, olive oil, and salt.

Fold parchment paper in half. Working in one direction, fold the edges tightly inwards to completely seal in the beets into a parcel.

Bake for 25 minutes then remove from the oven. Allow beets to continue steaming for 5 minutes before opening the parcel.

FOR THE RISOTTO

While the beets cook, make the risotto. Wipe out the Dutch oven.

Add shallots to the Dutch oven along with vinegar, olive oil, salt, miso, and rice.

Bring mixture to a simmer and cook for 5 minutes, stirring frequently. Add stock and return to a simmer. Cover and place Dutch oven in the oven. Cook for 20 minutes.

Remove from oven and keep covered for 10 minutes to allow rice to steam.

Stir in half of pumpkin seed "ricotta."

Top with beets, remaining pumpkin seed "ricotta," toasted pumpkin seeds, and greens.

Root Vegetable-Tater Tot Gratin

SERVES 4

Surprise! Tater tots don't just exist in the supermarket freezer section— you can make them yourself. These root-vegetable tots are more satisfying and delicious. To make this into a complete meal, add some sautéed kale or a side salad.

GATHER

ROOT-VEGETABLE TATER TOTS

	Oil or cooking spray, for greasing pan
2	cups peeled and diced sweet potatoes
1	cup peeled and diced carrots
8	cups water
1	tablespoon garlic powder
½	teaspoon sea salt
1½	cups finely grated Parmesan cheese, divided, more for garnish

GRATIN SAUCE

1	cup rolled oats, rinsed
4	cups filtered water
2	shallots, diced (approximately 1 cup)
⅓	cup white wine vinegar
3	tablespoons olive oil
4	teaspoons sea salt
2	(15-ounce) cans white beans (approximately 4 cups), drained and rinsed)
2	tablespoons fresh thyme leaves, more for garnish
¼	teaspoon ground black pepper, more for garnish
1	tablespoon maple syrup

MAKE IT

FOR THE TATER TOTS

Preheat oven to 425°F.

Line baking tray with parchment paper. Grease paper with oil or cooking spray.

Add sweet potatoes and carrots to medium to large Dutch oven along with water. Cover with a lid and bring to a boil. Cook for 10 minutes or until al dente.

Drain cooked vegetables. Spread onto towel to absorb any extra moisture and cool. Rinse out Dutch oven.

Once vegetables are cool, place in a large bowl and mash roughly with a fork. (Some larger pieces are okay.) Fold in garlic powder, salt, and 1 cup of the Parmesan.

Scoop tablespoon-size amounts of the mixture and form into a cylindrical tater tot shape. Roll tater tots in the remaining cheese and arrange in an evenly spaced single layer on prepared tray.

Bake for 20 minutes or until firm and golden on the bottom.

FOR THE GRATIN SAUCE

Add oats to a blender, along with filtered water. Blend for 20 seconds. Strain through fine-mesh bag or cheesecloth to yield oat "milk." Set aside.

Add shallots, vinegar, olive oil, and salt to Dutch oven and cook over low heat for 10 minutes or until most of the vinegar has evaporated. Add beans along with thyme and pepper. Turn up heat to medium and cook for additional 5 minutes.

Add oat "milk," bring to a simmer, and cook for additional 10 minutes, stirring occasionally. Turn off heat and fold in maple syrup.

Ladle sauce into bowls and top with tater tots, grated Parmesan, more thyme leaves, and black pepper.

Crispy Tofu and Cauliflower Coconut Curry

SERVES 4

You can substitute or add most any vegetables to this dish including carrots, zucchini, or kale. I suggest serving it with cooked brown rice. It also freezes well.

GATHER

- 1 (15-ounce) package organic firm tofu, pressed
- 3 tablespoons extra virgin olive oil, divided
- 1 large onion, finely diced
- 1 teaspoon turmeric powder
- 1 teaspoon kosher salt, divided
- 1 cup green beans, cut into 1½-inch pieces
- 1 red bell pepper, cut into 1-inch dice (approximately ½ cup)
- ½ head cauliflower, cut into florets (approximately 2 cups)
- ½ teaspoon freshly ground black pepper
- 2 (13-ounce) cans coconut milk (approximately 3 cups)
- 4 to 5 tablespoons red curry paste Cooked brown rice (optional) Thai basil, more for garnish

MAKE IT

Cut the pressed tofu into ¾-inch cubes.

Heat 1 tablespoon olive oil in a medium to large Dutch oven over medium-high heat.

When the oil is hot (but not smoking), put in the tofu. (It should sizzle.) Do not toss the tofu immediately. Allow it to get crispy and browned on one side before you flip it using a spatula, about 3 minutes. Continue to fry until all sides are golden. Remove the tofu from the pot and set aside.

To the same pot, add 1 more tablespoon olive oil, heat again, and add the onion. Lower the heat to medium and sauté for about 5 minutes or until translucent.

Add the remaining olive oil, turmeric, ½ teaspoon salt, green beans, bell pepper, cauliflower, and pepper and sauté for 5 more minutes.

Finally add the coconut milk, curry paste, tofu, and remaining salt. Bring to a boil, lower the heat, and simmer for another 18 or so minutes, or until the cauliflower and green beans are cooked to your liking.

Serve over rice, if desired, and garnish with Thai basil.

Cauli-Mushroom Risotto

SERVES 2

This cauliflower-centric take on risotto is both tasty and packed with nutrition. And it's vegan to boot. My friend Elizabeth Stein, founder of the wildly popular food brand Purely Elizabeth, created this one and says, "the cashew cream sauce is a great base for any dairy-free, cheesy sauce replacement."

GATHER

CASHEW CREAM
1 cup cashews, soaked
¼ cup coconut cream
¼ cup filtered water
1 lemon, juiced
¼ cup nutritional yeast

RISOTTO
2 tablespoons olive oil
1 shallot, diced
8 ounces mushrooms (such as maitake or shiitake), chopped
16 ounces cauliflower rice
1 cup vegetable broth, divided
  Salt
  Freshly ground black pepper

MAKE IT

To a high-speed blender, add cashews, coconut cream, water, lemon juice, and nutritional yeast, and blend until smooth.

Meanwhile, in a large skillet or Dutch oven over low to medium heat, add olive oil and shallot. Sauté for 3–5 minutes or until browned.

Add mushrooms and continue to sauté for 5–7 minutes or until browned. Add cauliflower rice and sauté for 3–5 minutes.

In ¼ cup increments, add vegetable broth and sauté until absorbed before adding more. Continue to add broth until 1 cup has been added.

Add desired amount of cashew cream and stir to combine.

Season with salt and pepper to taste and serve.

Jalapeño-Cheddar Grits with Poached Eggs

SERVES 2

Okay, yes you need a separate pot to poach the eggs, but this one still works because the spicy cheddar grits are delicious all on their own. If poaching eggs isn't your thing, you can also pan-fry them in a little butter or olive oil and rest them on top. The magic is in the runny yolk, so be sure to ladle this into big bowls.

GATHER

3	tablespoons unsalted grass-fed butter
2	jalapeños, sliced into thin rings
1	cup corn grits
2	teaspoons sea salt
10	cups filtered water, divided
4	organic eggs
2	cups grated cheddar cheese

MAKE IT

Heat butter in a large saucepan over medium heat. Add the jalapeño slices and cook until golden. Carefully remove a few slices from butter to reserve as garnish.

Stir the grits and salt into the jalapeño-butter mixture. Toast for 2–3 minutes, stirring occasionally.

Pour in 6 cups of water and stir until combined. Bring mixture to a simmer and cook for 25–30 minutes, or until tender.

In the meantime, bring remaining water to a light simmer in a separate pot. Gently crack in the eggs, and poach for 2–3 minutes, or until the whites have set.

Once the grits are cooked, stir in cheese until melted. Serve grits in bowls and top with poached eggs and reserved jalapeño slices.

Winter Scalloped Sweet Potato and Kale Gratin with Almond "Parmesan"

MAKES 1 (8-INCH) GRATIN

This recipe came from the Winter 2016 issue of *Naturally* and was focused on hero ingredients that can help you glow from the inside out. In this recipe, sweet potatoes are the hero ingredient that will supercharge your hair and skin. Your body converts the beta carotene in sweet potatoes to vitamin A, which is necessary for cell growth and renewal and can keep your hair strong and shiny.

GATHER

ALMOND "BÉCHAMEL"

½ cup blanched almonds, soaked

3 cups filtered water

¼ teaspoon ground nutmeg

2 tablespoons arrowroot starch

1 teaspoon garlic powder

½ teaspoon sea salt

1 lemon juiced (approximately 2 tablespoons)

ALMOND "PARMESAN"

½ cup almond flour

½ teaspoon sea salt

1 tablespoon miso

2 tablespoons refined coconut oil

WINTER GRATIN

1 bunch curly kale, stemmed and cut into thin ribbons

½ teaspoon sea salt

2 tablespoons refined coconut oil

3 medium sweet potatoes (about 2 pounds), peeled and thinly sliced

MAKE IT

FOR THE "BÉCHAMEL"

Blend soaked almonds and water in a high-speed blender. Strain through a fine-mesh sieve or cheesecloth.

Transfer to medium saucepan along with nutmeg, arrowroot, garlic powder, salt, and lemon juice. Bring to a boil, and turn heat off. Mixture should be thick.

FOR THE "PARMESAN"

Combine all ingredients in a bowl and rub together with your fingers until it is the texture of a coarse meal.

FOR THE GRATIN

Preheat oven to 350°F.

In a bowl, massage kale with salt until tender.

Coat an 8-inch gratin dish with coconut oil. Create gratin layers by alternating sweet potatoes, kale, and a ladleful of "béchamel." Repeat until gratin is finished. Sprinkle with "Parmesan."

Bake for 45 minutes or until potatoes are tender and top is golden.

Kale and Goat Cheese Frittata

MAKES 1 (8-INCH) FRITTATA

Kale is loaded with lutein, which keeps your eyes sparkling (and healthy). It also contains vitamin C, which is vital for skin health. Finally, kale trumps others in the fiber department and leads by a long shot with vitamins A, C, and K, blowing spinach out of the salad spinner.

GATHER

- 4 tablespoons refined coconut oil, divided
- 1 medium yellow onion, sliced
- 1¼ teaspoons sea salt, divided
- ½ pound kale, stemmed and cut into thin ribbons
- 8 organic eggs
- ¼ cup goat cheese, crumbled
- ½ teaspoon freshly ground black pepper

MAKE IT

In a medium sauté pan, heat 2 tablespoons of the oil. Add onion and ½ teaspoon salt and cook until translucent, 4–5 minutes, stirring occasionally.

In a large bowl, massage kale with ½ teaspoon salt until tender.

Preheat oven to 375°F, and warm a cast iron or other oven-safe skillet for 5 minutes.

In a separate bowl, whisk eggs and fold in the kale, onion, cheese, pepper, and remaining sea salt.

Coat warmed skillet with remaining oil. Pour in egg mixture. Place in the oven and cook until set, about 8 minutes.

Cauliflower-Yogurt Grits with Balsamic-Glazed Root Vegetables

SERVES 2 TO 4

Traditional grits are made with cornmeal and are carb bombs. Since they're made from starchy corn, the high carbohydrate count means they're also loaded in sugar (and not to mention the fat from the butter and cheese that is normally added to make grits so gosh darn good).

This is our somewhat controversial take on grits. Instead of cornmeal, we replace it with grated cauliflower, and the end result is creamy and tasty. But if you miss the exact mouthfeel of traditional grits, meet me in the middle: split the difference between cornmeal and cauliflower. You'll get all the nutrition and cut the carbs in half.

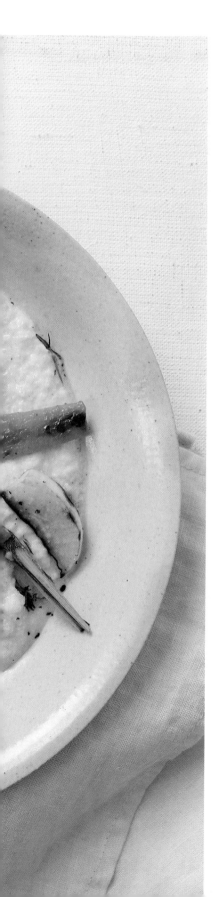

GATHER

BALSAMIC-GLAZED ROOT VEGETABLES

1   bunch carrots
1   bunch baby turnips, peeled and quartered lengthwise
2   tablespoons olive oil
½   teaspoon sea salt
2   tablespoons balsamic vinegar
2   sprigs thyme leaves

CAULIFLOWER-YOGURT GRITS

2   tablespoons olive oil
1   yellow onion, diced small (approximately 1½ cups)
1½ teaspoons sea salt
1   small head cauliflower, grated on the large side of a box grater
3   tablespoons nutritional yeast
1   (13.5-ounce) can coconut milk (approximately 2 cups)
1½ cups Greek yogurt

MAKE IT

FOR THE BALSAMIC-GLAZED ROOT VEGETABLES

Preheat oven to 350°F. Line a baking tray with parchment paper.

Peel and quarter carrots lengthwise, leaving 1 inch of greens attached.

Toss the turnips and carrots with the olive oil and salt. Spread on the prepared tray and roast for 20 minutes.

Toss vegetables with vinegar and roast for additional 5 minutes.

FOR THE CAULIFLOWER-YOGURT GRITS

While the vegetables roast, prepare the grits. Add the oil to a medium pot over medium heat. Add the onion and salt. Cook onion for 3–5 minutes, stirring occasionally. Add cauliflower and cook for an additional 2 minutes.

Stir in nutritional yeast and coconut milk and bring mixture to a simmer. Reduce heat, cover, and simmer for 10 minutes or until tender and creamy, stirring every few minutes to prevent mixture from scorching at the bottom of the pot.

Transfer 2 cups of the cauliflower mixture into a blender along with the yogurt, and blend until smooth. Return to pot, and rewarm, taking care not to boil.

Serve the grits topped with the glazed root vegetables and a sprinkling of thyme leaves.

Carrot Risotto with Macadamia "Parmesan"

SERVES 4

I make this recipe all the time because I still haven't found a person who hasn't licked their plate clean. The sweetness that comes from the roasted carrots and the nuttiness that shines through from the macadamia nuts and nutritional yeast just play so well with the fragrant jasmine rice.

GATHER

MACADAMIA "PARMESAN"

¼	cup macadamia nuts
1	tablespoon nutritional yeast
¼	teaspoon sea salt
2	teaspoons olive oil

CARROT RISOTTO

1	bunch carrots with tops (approximately 6 medium)
2	tablespoons olive oil
1	medium onion
1½	cups jasmine rice
4	cups vegetable broth
3	cloves garlic
3	tablespoons nutritional yeast
1	tablespoon sea salt
2	tablespoons white wine vinegar
1½	cups filtered warm water, more to thin

MAKE IT

FOR THE "PARMESAN"

Finely grate macadamia nuts into a small bowl. Toss with yeast, salt, and olive oil. Set aside.

FOR THE CARROT RISOTTO

Preheat oven to 425°F. Line a baking tray with parchment paper.

Trim and peel carrots, leaving 1 inch of the greens intact. Reserve a few carrot greens for garnish. Cut carrot tops and split in half. Cut remaining carrots into rounds and toss with olive oil.

Slice onion and add to carrot mixture. Spread on prepared baking tray, cover tightly with foil, and roast for 25 minutes or until tender.

In the meantime add rice and broth to a medium pot. Bring mixture to a simmer over low heat, and stir frequently for 10–15 minutes or until cooked through. Turn off heat and cover to keep warm.

Remove vegetables from the oven and set aside roasted carrot tops. Add the remaining mixture to a blender along with the garlic, nutritional yeast, salt, vinegar, and water and blend until smooth. Add more water if the mixture is too thick.

Add carrot purée and half of macadamia "Parmesan" to cooked jasmine rice, stirring to combine.

To serve, place risotto in each bowl and garnish with macadamia "Parmesan," carrot greens, and roasted carrot tops.

Chipotle Sweet Potato Gratin

SERVES 6 LARGE

Food and craft blogger Mary Helen Leonard shares this pure comfort-food recipe from the Spring 2018 issue of *Naturally*. This one is definitely a good option for a special holiday and really dresses up sweet potatoes in a more complex way by using smoky chipotle peppers and a creamy cheese sauce. Did we mention it's quick and easy? Serve it on a quinoa salad base for an extra protein boost.

GATHER

- 1 cup heavy cream
- 1 cup Mexican crema or sour cream
- ½ teaspoon garlic powder
- ½ teaspoon salt
- ¼ teaspoon black pepper
- 1 (7-ounce) can chipotle peppers in adobo
- 2 pounds sweet potatoes, peeled and thinly sliced
- 8 ounces Monterey jack cheese, grated
- 2 tablespoons minced fresh chives or freeze-dried chives

MAKE IT

Preheat oven to 400°F.

Combine heavy cream, crema, garlic powder, salt, and pepper in small food processor or blender. Add chipotle peppers to taste (1 pepper for mild, 2–3 for medium, 3–4 for hot). Add a dollop (1 to 3 teaspoons) of sauce from the can as well. Purée until smooth.

Place one layer of sliced sweet potatoes into casserole dish, then drizzle ¼ to ½ cup of cream mixture and a handful of cheese over the top. Continue making layers until all of the ingredients are used. Sprinkle the top layer with chives.

Bake for 45–50 minutes, or until sweet potatoes are tender. Let sit for 5–10 minutes before serving.

Spring Vegetable–Fried Sorghum with Baked Eggs

SERVES 4

Sorghum is a superstar grain. It's naturally gluten-free and loaded with good fat, protein, fiber, and has more antioxidants than blueberries and pomegranates.

GATHER

1 cup sorghum, rinsed

3 cups filtered water

3 tablespoons hot sesame oil, divided

4 organic eggs

1¼ teaspoons sea salt, divided

1 large red onion, sliced into thin rings

1 cup snap peas, strings removed and cut into half diagonally

MAKE IT

Place sorghum and filtered water into a small saucepan and bring to a simmer over medium heat. Reduce heat and cook for 45 minutes, or until tender. Drain any remaining water and allow sorghum to cool slightly.

Preheat oven to 350°F. Brush the inside of 4 cupcake pan cavities (or ovenproof ramekins) with 1 tablespoon oil.

Crack 1 egg into each cavity and sprinkle with ¼ teaspoon salt, evenly divided, over the 4 eggs. Bake for 12 minutes, or until the whites of the eggs have set.

While the eggs bake, heat remaining sesame oil in wok or large pan. Add onion rings and remaining salt to the oil, and cook for 2–4 minutes, or until softened. Stir frequently.

Fold in cooked sorghum and cook for 2 additional minutes. Add snap peas and cook for additional minute.

Plate fried sorghum into bowls and top each serving with a baked egg.

Brûléed Pumpkin Mac and Cheese

SERVES 4

GATHER

- 1 tablespoon plus ½ teaspoon sea salt, divided
- 1 tablespoon olive oil
- 1 (8-ounce) package macaroni
- 2 tablespoons grass-fed butter, more for greasing dish
- 2 tablespoons flour
- 1 cup milk
- 1 cup grated sharp cheddar cheese
- 1 cup pumpkin purée
  Pinch of nutmeg

MAKE IT

Preheat oven to 375°F. Bring a medium pot filled halfway with water to a boil, and season water with 1 tablespoon salt and the olive oil. Add macaroni and cook for 8–10 minutes, or until al dente.

In a medium saucepan over medium heat, melt the butter and stir in the flour. Cook for 2–3 minutes, stirring constantly. Add the milk and cheese, bring to a boil, and cook for 1 minute. Fold in the pumpkin, remaining salt, nutmeg, and cooked macaroni.

Grease oven-safe dish with butter. Transfer mixture to dish and bake for 20–30 minutes, or until golden, hot, and bubbly.

Toasted Sesame and Maple Caramelized Tofu

SERVES 2

GATHER

1   block firm tofu, pressed
2   tablespoons toasted sesame oil
3   cloves garlic, minced
3   tablespoons maple syrup
½   cup apple juice
2   tablespoons tamari
1   (1-inch) piece ginger, peeled and minced
2   scallions, sliced

MAKE IT

Preheat oven to 375°F.

Cut the pressed tofu width-wise into 3 even slabs. Quarter each third to form 12 triangles in total. Arrange tofu in a single layer in a baking dish.

In a medium bowl, whisk together the sesame oil, garlic, syrup, juice, tamari, and ginger. Pour mixture over tofu and allow to marinate for 15–30 minutes.

Bake, uncovered, for 30–40 minutes, turning once. Tofu should absorb most of the liquid and turn golden.

Garnish with sliced scallions.

Saffron Quinoa "Paella" with Kalamata Olives

SERVES 4

This is a great recipe to clean out the fridge. Add lots of veggies to this and turn it into stir-fry. Wilted greens, diced potatoes, and even fresh tomatoes all lend well to this protein- and fiber-rich take on paella.

GATHER

1	teaspoon saffron
1	bunch cilantro
3	tablespoons olive oil
1	cup pearl onions, peeled and quartered lengthwise
2	cups quinoa
1½	teaspoons sea salt
3½	cups filtered water
½	cup pitted Kalamata olives
1	cup sliced almonds, divided

MAKE IT

Bloom saffron by placing in a few tablespoons of hot water for 15 minutes.

Remove stems from cilantro, chop leaves, and tie stems together with twine.

Warm olive oil in medium pan. Add pearl onions and cook for 2 minutes, or until golden and blistered.

Add in quinoa and salt and continue to toast for additional minute. Add filtered water, tied cilantro stems, and bloomed saffron to a large pan. Bring to a simmer, reduce heat to low, cover, and cook for 15 minutes.

Remove from heat and leave pot covered to steam for 5 minutes. Discard cilantro stems.

Toss with chopped cilantro leaves (approximately ⅓ cup) and ½ cup almonds. Top with olives and remaining sliced almonds, to serve.

Maple-Miso Baked Beans with Blistered Shishitos

SERVES 4

The earthy, saltiness of the miso and the sweet maple syrup are in flavor-combination heaven in this recipe. If you don't have a Dutch oven, a cast iron skillet covered in aluminum foil will do.

GATHER

MAPLE-MISO BAKED BEANS

- 3 tablespoons maple syrup
- 3 tablespoons white miso
- 1 tablespoon Dijon mustard
- 3 tablespoons apple cider vinegar
- 1 teaspoon liquid smoke
- 2 teaspoons sea salt
- 2 cups vegetable stock
- ¼ cup olive oil
- 4 scallions
- 3 (14.5-ounce) cans (or 6 cups cooked) black beans, drained and rinsed

BLISTERED SHISHITOS

- 2 tablespoons olive oil
- 16 shishito peppers (8 ounces)
- 1 teaspoon flaky salt, for serving

MAKE IT

FOR THE BAKED BEANS

Preheat oven to 450°F.

In a large bowl, whisk together maple syrup, miso, mustard, vinegar, liquid smoke, salt, stock, and olive oil.

Cut scallions into slices. Add white parts to marinade, and reserve greens for garnish.

Gently fold beans into marinade. Transfer mixture to a medium to large Dutch oven. Bring beans to a simmer over medium heat. Boil for 2 minutes.

Carefully transfer Dutch oven to oven and cook, uncovered, for 20 minutes. Remove from oven and allow to cool for a few minutes.

Stir in sliced scallion greens.

FOR THE SHISHITOS

Heat a medium pan over high heat for 2 minutes.

Add olive oil, directly followed by peppers, and cook for 2 minutes per side, or until blistered. Note: Peppers can possibly burst. If too much splattering occurs, carefully place a lid on the pan, step away, and turn off heat for 30 seconds before continuing the blistering process.

Place the shishitos on top of the baked beans and sprinkle with salt before serving.

HAPPY ENDINGS

Yes, this is a book about dinnertime. But is there anything better than having a little something sweet to round out a delicious meal?

If you loved my previous book, *Naturally, Delicious Desserts,* you're going to love these bonus dessert recipes. I wanted to add these as a bit of surprise that both delights and reaffirms that, yes, dessert can still be good for you.

As I've gotten older, my taste for sweets has evolved, too. Gone are the days I relished in heavily frosted cake slices or chocolate sauce–covered sundaes with sugary toppings. Now, I like things that are a little sweet or allow fresh ingredients like fruit to shine when they are at their peak of perfection. Or maybe it's a lightly sweetened meringue, so it has all those perfect textures and flavors working together: chewy, crunchy, and sweet.

If I had to do a shout-out to my favorite recipe in this bunch, it's hands down our healthy take on "Eggos" (page 198). We loaded it up with good-for-you ingredients such as lentils, brown rice, and probiotic powder, and then we shared a tip about how to freeze leftover waffles and toast them up right out of the freezer. For me, when our waffle is crispy and hot, a spoonful of peanut butter and a little dollop of vanilla ice cream is all you need for a quick and incredible sweet sensation.

Collagen-Marbled Assorted Fruit Leathers

MAKES 3 (12 X 12-INCH) FRUIT LEATHER SHEETS

Here's something fruity, chewy, and full of good-for-you collagen that can help boost your bones, plump your skin, and even fortify your muscles. While most collagen powders are bovine derived, you can find vegan alternatives that deliver similar results. For this recipe, we chose applesauce as the base because of the abundant pectin already in it, which helps bind and create the "leather" as it dehydrates.

GATHER

BASE FOR EACH FLAVOR

2   tablespoons lemon juice
½   cup unsweetened applesauce
2   tablespoons collagen powder

FRUIT VARIATIONS

1   cup frozen strawberries
1   cup frozen pink dragon fruit
1   cup frozen mango

MAKE IT

Line 3 dehydrator trays with designated nonstick silicone mats.

Add lemon juice, apple sauce, and collagen powder to a blender and process until smooth. Choose one of the fruit variations, add to blender, and process until smooth. Transfer to a bowl.

Rinse out the blender or food processor. Repeat process with remaining fruit variations.

Choose a fruit variation and use an offset spatula to spread into a thin layer onto one of the trays, reserving ¼ cup to use to top another tray.

Spoon the reserved purée of a different fruit variation on top in a swirling pattern. Drag the back of a spoon, repeatedly, to form the shape of a number 8 to create the marbled effect.

Dehydrate the trays for 6–8 hours at 130°F, or until fruit leathers easily peel off the silicone mats.

Cut into desired shapes using kitchen shears and enjoy.

If storing for extended amount of time, place onto parchment paper, roll, and secure. Store in an airtight container to keep leathers from drying out.

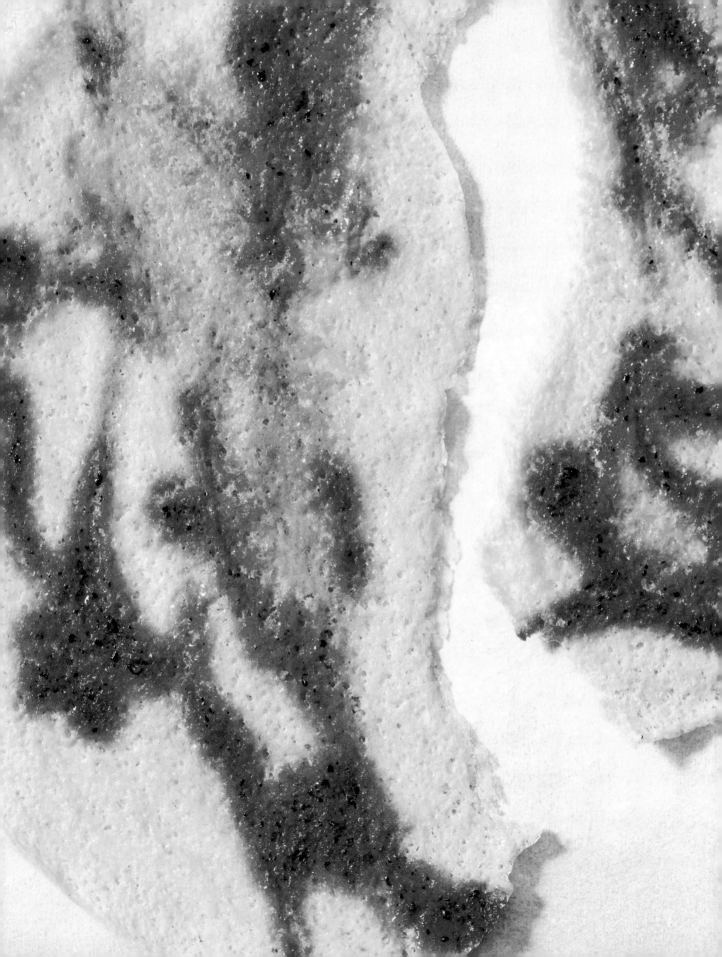

Overnight "Sourdough Eggos" with "Magic Shell" Chocolate-Drizzled Frozen Berries

MAKES 4 CUPS BATTER; 12 WAFFLES; 3 CUPS BERRY TOPPING

Just like the supermarket variety, leftover waffles can be frozen and reheated right out of the freezer in a toaster oven. Just be sure the waffles are completely cool before transferring to an airtight container. Place in a toaster for 2 minutes to heat them up.

GATHER

"MAGIC SHELL" CHOCOLATE-DRIZZLED FROZEN BERRIES

- 2 cups frozen mixed berries
- 2 tablespoons refined coconut oil
- 1 cup dark chocolate chips

SOURDOUGH "EGGOS"

- ½ cup dried red lentils
- ½ cup short-grain brown rice
- 1 teaspoon probiotic powder
- 1 tablespoon vanilla extract
- 3 tablespoons maple syrup, more to serve
  Pinch sea salt
- 1 cup spelt flour
- 1½ teaspoons baking powder
- ¼ cup refined coconut oil
- 2 tablespoons organic confectioners' sugar, for serving (optional)

MAKE IT

FOR THE FROZEN BERRIES

Line a baking tray with parchment paper. Place frozen berries in a single layer.

Warm coconut oil in a pan over low heat until melted. Slowly stir in the chocolate chips, stirring frequently until melted.

Drizzle chocolate mixture on berries and place in freezer until solid. Use hands to break into smaller pieces and store frozen in a container until ready to use as topping.

FOR THE "EGGOS"

Add lentils and rice to a pot. Cover with water and bring to a boil. Shut off heat and allow mixture to sit for 10 minutes.

Drain lentil-and-rice mixture and add to a blender along with 1½ cups water. Blend for 1 minute, or until completely smooth.

Transfer to a bowl and stir in probiotic powder. Cover mixture and allow batter to ferment for 2 hours, or overnight in the refrigerator.

Fold in vanilla, syrup, salt, flour, and baking powder.

Melt coconut oil. Stir 2 tablespoons into batter, and use remaining oil to grease waffle maker in between waffles.

Pour batter into waffle maker. Cook for 3–5 minutes or until golden and cooked through. (Note: the interior of waffles will be soft when preliminarily cooked but will crisp up more once frozen and reheated in toaster or oven.)

Dust finished "Eggos" with confectioners' sugar, if using, and top with berries.

Cuyama Buckhorn Dutch Baby Pancake

MAKES 1 LARGE
PANCAKE

This recipe comes to us from the most unexpected place: the Cuyama Buckhorn motel. It's in the middle of nowhere, between Bakersfield and Santa Maria in California. But being nowhere doesn't mean it isn't magical: If you get there at the right time, massive carpets of wildflowers bloom known as a "superbloom" around you in an absolute epic Instagram-worthy moment. The chef from Cuyama Buckhorn shared this cast iron favorite so you don't have to make the trek out West.

GATHER

DUTCH BABY PANCAKE

- 3 tablespoons grass-fed unsalted butter
- 3 organic eggs
- ¾ cup all-purpose flour
- ¾ cup milk, warm
- 1 tablespoon sugar
- ½ teaspoon vanilla extract
- Pinch of salt

THYME-ROASTED APRICOT CHUTNEY

- 1 pound apricots, halved and pitted
- 5 sprigs thyme
- 2 cups sugar
- 3 tablespoons apple cider vinegar
- Pinch of salt

HONEY CRÈME

- 1 cup heavy whipping cream
- ¼ cup honey
- 3 tablespoons confectioners' sugar
- Pinch of salt

MAKE IT

FOR THE PANCAKE

Preheat oven to 400°F.

Put the butter in a large, ovenproof, nonstick sauté pan and place in the oven.

Meanwhile, in a blender, combine the eggs, flour, milk, sugar, vanilla, and salt, and blend on medium-high speed until uniform. (If mixing by hand, combine the eggs with the milk until the mixture is light yellow and no longer stringy, about 1 minute. Add the sugar and salt, and whisk vigorously to remove the lumps, about 30 seconds.)

Carefully remove the hot pan from the oven. The butter should be melted. Swirl the butter around the pan to coat completely, and then pour the remaining butter into the batter and pulse to blend.

Pour the batter into the hot pan and return the pan to the oven. Cook until the pancake is puffed in the center and golden brown along the edges, 20–25 minutes.

Using a spatula, remove the entire Dutch baby from the pan and place on a cooling rack for a few minutes to allow the steam to escape without condensing along the bottom and rendering the pancake soggy.

FOR THE CHUTNEY

Combine the apricots, thyme, sugar, vinegar, and salt in a pot over low heat, and let simmer until the apricots begin to caramelize. If syrup is too sweet add a little extra vinegar. Remove thyme sprigs before serving.

FOR THE HONEY CRÈME

Whisk or beat the cream, honey, sugar, and salt together until stiff peaks form.

To serve, slice the pancake into 8 wedges and top with the chutney and the crème.

Coconut Caramel Waffle Stack

MAKES 2 CUPS BATTER (4 TO 6 WAFFLES); 1 CUP CARAMEL

True fact: I like chocolate, but I don't *love* it. For me, sticky caramel is where it's at for my deserted island favorite dessert. And this waffle stack is incredible for Sunday brunch or for dessert. Warm waffles + vanilla ice cream = perfection. By the way, if you don't have a waffle iron, you can make pancakes with this batter.

GATHER

WAFFLES

1½	cups dairy-free milk
2	organic eggs
1½	cups gluten-free flour (such as Bob's Red Mill All-Purpose Baking Blend)
1½	teaspoons baking powder
2	tablespoons refined coconut oil, more to grease iron
	Pinch of sea salt

COCONUT CARAMEL

2	cups frozen pitted cherries, for topping
2½	cups nondairy milk
½	cup coconut sugar
2	tablespoons refined coconut oil

MAKE IT

WAFFLES

Add milk, eggs, flour, baking powder, oil, and salt to a blender and process until smooth. Allow to rest for 5 minutes.

Preheat waffle iron and grease lightly with coconut oil.

Working in batches, pour ¼ cup batter for each waffle and cook for 2–3 minutes, or until cooked through and golden.

CARAMEL

Take out cherries from freezer to defrost.

Add milk, sugar, and oil to a pan and bring to a simmer.

Cook for 12–15 minutes over high heat, stirring occasionally. Mixture should be glossy and thickened.

Pour caramel over waffles, and garnish with cherries before serving.

Mini Pancake Cereal Sundae

MAKES 1 ¼ CUPS "ICE CREAM"; 1 ¼ CUPS PANCAKE BATTER

This is one of the most adorable sundaes you can make for a crowd, and it uses just a few ingredients and has just a few steps! Use a full-fat nondairy milk for this recipe; the fat helps give it a richness that it deserves. If you have a nut allergy, you can use a nut-free milk made from ingredients like banana or hemp.

GATHER

NO-CHURN "ICE CREAM"
½ cup cashews
3 cups almond milk
¼ cup refined coconut oil

MINI PANCAKES
1 cup almond milk
1½ teaspoons baking powder
1 cup oat flour
1 banana
2 tablespoons refined coconut oil, more to grease pan
Toasted pecans, for garnish

MAKE IT

FOR THE "ICE CREAM"
Add cashews and milk to a pan and bring to a boil. Boil for 15 minutes over high heat. Approximately ¾ cup of milk mixture should remain. Cool slightly.

Add milk mixture and oil to a blender and process for 1 minute or until mixture is completely smooth.

Place in a shallow container and freeze for 2 hours or until firm.

FOR THE PANCAKES
Add milk, baking powder, flour, banana, and oil to a blender. Process until smooth. Transfer batter to a squeeze bottle.

Lightly grease a nonstick pan, and heat over medium heat.

Squeeze small dollops of batter onto pan and cook for 1 minute per side or until cooked through. Repeat with remaining batter.

Serve with pecans and "ice cream."

Winter Banana Nog

SERVES 4

Dates are such a wonderful sugar-free sweetener because they are delicious and good for you! They are rich in antioxidants that support brain, eye, and heart health. This recipe comes from The Ranch Malibu, a high-end health and wellness resort known for helping people reboot their personal health. Sure, it's a "winter" nog, but you can drink this any time of the year.

GATHER

2	large ripe bananas
2	cups vanilla coconut yogurt
8	to 10 Medjool dates, halved and pitted
2	generous pinches of freshly grated nutmeg
2	pinches of sea salt, more to taste
2	cups ice

MAKE IT

Place all of the ingredients into a blender. Blend on high, adding the ice cubes until completely smooth. Add 1–2 tablespoons of cold water if needed to adjust consistency and an additional pinch of salt to taste, if desired.

Sparkling Pomegranate-Kombucha Granita

MAKES 8 CUPS

Between the ginger, pomegranate juice, and kombucha, this is one zingy recipe your taste buds will love.

GATHER

1	(2-inch) piece ginger
4	cups pomegranate juice
½	cup raw honey (optional)
2	cups kombucha
	Pomegranate seeds (optional)

MAKE IT

Peel ginger and roughly cut into chunks.

Add cut ginger, juice, and honey, if using, to blender and process until smooth.

Pass through a fine-mesh strainer to remove any residual ginger pulp. Stir in kombucha.

Transfer mixture to a wide, lidded, freezer-safe container. Cover and place in freezer.

Scrape every 60 minutes until the mixture forms into ice crystals. The process should take 2–4 hours. Serve with pomegranate seeds, if desired.

Pomegranate-Ginger Elixir Gummies

MAKES 1 CUP MIXTURE; APPROXIMATELY 48 (1-TEASPOON) GUMMIES

We're thinking this might be the most fun way to get those good pomegranate nutrients—from chews!

GATHER

- 1 (1-inch) piece ginger, peeled and cut into chunks
- 1 orange, juiced
- 1 cup pomegranate juice
- 2 tablespoons agave nectar (optional)
- ¼ cup agar agar flakes
  Sugar, for dusting

MAKE IT

Place ginger, orange juice, pomegranate juice, and agave nectar, if using, in a blender and process until smooth. Pass mixture through fine-mesh strainer into a small pan, discarding pulp.

Stir in agar agar flakes and allow to rehydrate for 5 minutes.

Place mixture over low heat and bring to a simmer. Cook for 5 minutes, stirring occasionally until agar agar flakes dissolve.

Cool mixture for a few minutes.

Pour into a shallow dish until about ½ inch to 1 inch full.

Chill in refrigerator for 30–60 minutes, or until set.

Cut into small cubes and dust in sugar.

Pomegranate-Citrus Aquafaba Pavlova

MAKES 1 (12-INCH)
PAVLOVA (3 CUPS BATTER)
AND 1 CUP CREAM

Named after Russian ballerina Anna Pavlova, this dessert is beautiful to behold and healthy to boot. A traditional Pavlova uses egg whites, but we made this totally plant-based using a surprise ingredient: chickpea liquid (aquafaba). Have fun with it! Slice up whatever fruit is fresh and in-season to give it a totally different flavor profile every time.

GATHER

2 (15-ounce) cans chickpeas
¼ teaspoon cream of tartar
½ cup organic cane sugar
3 oranges, zested
¾ cup cashews
2 tablespoons filtered water
1 tablespoon agave nectar
1 grapefruit
1 pomegranate

MAKE IT

Preheat oven to 250°F. Line a rimmed baking tray with parchment paper.

Drain chickpea liquid into a saucepan (approximately 1½ cups). Save chickpeas for another use. Cook over high heat until the liquid reduces to ½ cup, about 5 minutes. Cool mixture completely.

Place chickpea liquid and cream of tartar in a stand mixer or large bowl. Use whisk attachment or electric beaters to whip aquafaba on high speed for 2 minutes or until fluffy stiff peaks form, scraping down sides as needed.

Add in sugar, 1 tablespoon at a time, until mixture becomes glossy. Fold 2 teaspoons of orange zest into the batter, setting aside remainder.

Scoop mixture into pile on prepared try, using a spoon to smooth out into a 1-inch thickness that is approximately 10 inches wide.

Bake for 60–90 minutes or until Pavlova is hard to the touch. Leaving on parchment paper, transfer to a wire rack to cool. Note: Pavlova can stick to wire without parchment paper.

While the Pavlova bakes, prepare the toppings. Add cashews to a pan and cover with water. Bring to a boil. Cook for 10 minutes.

Juice 1 orange. Drain and add cashews to blender. Add ⅓ cup orange juice, filtered water, and agave nectar. Blend for 1 minute or until completely smooth. Fold in 1 teaspoon orange zest. Cover and refrigerate until ready to use.

Using a knife, cut off both ends of the remaining oranges and grapefruit. Peel and cut off remaining pith. Cut citrus into rounds.

Seed pomegranate by cutting in half and placing in water and using fingers to loosen out seeds (approximately 1 cup). Dry on a towel before using.

Top Pavlova with cashew cream, citrus rounds, and pomegranate seeds right before serving. Note: the center will sink a bit from the weight of the cream and fruit.

Mung Bean Pancake

SERVES 2 TO 3

Ayurvedic doctor Martha Soffer has been on a mission to help clients nourish their mind, body, and spirit. She says this high-protein treat is easily digested, highly nutritious, and naturally detoxifying because of one hero ingredient: mung beans. Martha says its best to top them with fresh fruit, coconut yogurt, and a drizzle of coconut nectar with fresh fruit.

GATHER

- ⅔ cup organic mung beans
- ⅓ cup organic basmati rice
- ⅛ teaspoon cinnamon
- 1 organic apple, pear, mango, or berries
  Refined coconut oil, ghee, or water
  Coconut nectar, for serving (optional)

MAKE IT

The day or night before you intend on eating these pancakes, wash the beans and the rice well. Mix together with hot water to cover and let soak overnight. Make sure there's room in the container you're using for the mixture to expand. Do not screw on or tighten any lids completely.

In the morning, dump out the water and rinse the rice and beans well. Add fresh water, filling the jar up to just under the grain mixture.

Combine the grains, the water, and the cinnamon in a blender and blend until it becomes a batter. Set aside.

Add sliced fruit and some coconut oil, ghee, or water to a pan. Simmer the fruit until it's soft and cooked all the way through.

In a separate pan, heat up a little coconut oil and cook the batter like a pancake.

Top the pancake with the cooked fruit and the coconut nectar, if desired.

Tofu and Pineapple Pie

SERVES 8

Yes, you can use tofu to make dessert. The trick is to use the right one. In this case, it's silken tofu, which is the softest of all tofu and easily falls apart. Because of this, it's ideal for anything where you want a smooth, creamy consistency. This tropical dream is not only tasty—it's vegan and packed with protein.

GATHER

8	ounces silken tofu
1½	cups raw cashews
1¼	cups frozen pineapple
¼	cup coconut cream
2	tablespoons maple syrup
4	dates, pitted
2	teaspoons ground turmeric
1	(9-inch) prebaked pie shell
	Fresh fruit, for garnish (optional)
	Toasted coconut, for garnish (optional)

MAKE IT

Put the tofu, cashews, pineapple, coconut cream, maple syrup, dates, and turmeric in a high-speed blender and process on high for 1 minute or until smooth and slightly thickened.

Using a spatula, transfer the cream mixture to the pie shell and spread evenly.

If there is extra filling, you can chill it in a glass and eat with fruit.

Chill pie in the freezer for about 4 hours or until firm.

Let the pie soften at room temperature for 15 minutes before serving.

If desired, garnish with a few slices of fresh fruit and toasted coconut.

Raw Pumpkin Cheesecake

SERVES 8

Here's a dessert that looks like it took you forever to make but didn't. The trick here is to use a fresh and delicious granola for the crust. Changing up the kind of the granola will give you a totally different flavor every time.

GATHER

CRUST

1	(8-ounce) bag granola (such as Purely Elizabeth Honey Almond Probiotic Granola)
⅓	cup refined coconut oil

FOR THE FILLING

1½	cups cashews, soaked in water for 3 hours
3	tablespoons maple syrup
¼	cup refined coconut oil
¼	cup pumpkin purée
1	teaspoon pumpkin spice

MAKE IT

Grind the granola and coconut oil in a food processor. Press the dough into a tart pan and freeze.

Meanwhile, to the blender, add the drained cashews, maple syrup, coconut oil, pumpkin purée and pumpkin pie spice, and blend until smooth. Pour over the crust and freeze until set.

Let the cheesecake soften at room temperature for 15 minutes before serving.

If desired, garnish with blackberries and granola.

INDEX

ABOUT THE AUTHOR

Danny Seo is the editor in chief of *Naturally, Danny Seo*, a national print magazine that celebrates the idea that style and sustainability don't need to be mutually exclusive from each other. *Naturally, Delicious Dinners* is his twelfth book and his third cookbook, following the hit success *Naturally, Delicious*. Danny was the host of the Emmy Award-winning TV show *Naturally, Danny Seo* on NBC, which brought all of the ideas for cooking, home decorating, beauty, wellness, and travel to life that you see in the pages of his magazine. His line of eco-friendly products is sold in stores across the United States, Canada, and Europe, including retailers like TJ Maxx, Marshalls, and HomeGoods. He lives in Bucks County, Pennsylvania.

Metric Conversion Chart

VOLUME MEASUREMENTS		WEIGHT MEASUREMENTS		TEMPERATURE CONVERSION	
U.S.	METRIC	U.S.	METRIC	FAHRENHEIT	CELSIUS
1 teaspoon	5 ml	1/2 ounce	15 g	250	120
1 tablespoon	15 ml	1 ounce	30 g	300	150
1/4 cup	60 ml	3 ounces	90 g	325	160
1/3 cup	75 ml	4 ounces	115 g	350	180
1/2 cup	125 ml	8 ounces	225 g	375	190
2/3 cup	150 ml	12 ounces	350 g	400	200
3/4 cup	175 ml	1 pound	450 g	425	220
1 cup	250 ml	2 1/4 pounds	1 kg	450	230